50
HIKING TRAILS

LASSEN TAHOE CARSON PASS

By Don & Roberta Lowe

The Touchstone Press
P.O. Box 81
Beaverton, Oregon 97075

I.S.B.N. No. 0-911518-74-6

Bumpass Hell

Round Top from near Winnemucca Lake

introduction

In many ways the Lassen Peak and Lake Tahoe areas have much in common. Their grandiose mountainous terrain is ribboned with trails, a majority of which interconnect. The everchanging scenery ranges from woods of assorted compositions through meadows of varied size to vast, open ridges past exquisite timberline settings to barren summits. Hundreds of lakes, from those tucked in steep walled cirques to ones sprawled on valley floors, dot the surface. A few of those lakes would be top contenders for the best mountain swimming holes in the Western hemisphere and dozens more rate a B+. Even wildflowers connect the two areas—the raucous yellow blooms of wyethia, also called mule ears, cover many open slopes and the refreshing minty scent of pennyroyal (the leaves of which make a tasty tea) perfumes the air. And of course, there's always lupine in one of its many guises. Up to 80 species thrive in California, from sea level to 11,000 feet. Another, perhaps not quite so welcome, characteristic the Lassen Peak and Lake Tahoe areas share is that they are not the places to be if you're seeking solitude. Exceptional scenery and many trails combined with their proximity to large cities make such heavy use inevitable, especially in the Lake Tahoe area. But minimizing the effect of many people is the expansive nature of the terrain plus the civilized, unobtrusive conduct of most people who hike the trails. Most likely you'll get used to seeing fellow travelers and, in fact, may become a little apprehensive about what exactly is going on back down there in civilization when you don't see them for long periods of time. On trip No. 30 the paraphernalia from the Squaw Valley Ski Area is ever visible. However, the scenery is so grand you can just pretend you're hiking in Switzerland. As a reward for that attitude you can enjoy a proper European lunch on the deck, called High Camp, of the aerial tram's upper terminal.

But the one characteristic that the Lassen Peak area and the terrain to the south don't share is a major one: They each are part of separate mountain systems and are geologically unrelated. The southern boundary of the Park is the very end of the Cascades, that volcanic range extending north through Oregon and Washington and into Canada. Just a very few miles away—a couple of paces in the big scheme of things—at the north end of Lake Almanor is the beginning of the Sierra Nevada. (Actually, the Klamath Mountains in northwestern California are related to the Sierra, but that's another story.)

In the Lassen Peak section all the trails are in the Park with the exception of the two in the Caribou Wilderness (No's. 15 and 16). If someone tried to create a text book perfect example of vulcanism he couldn't have done better than what Lassen offers. It's all there: plug and shield volcanoes, cinder cones, immense lava flows, volcanic ash and, most spectacular, the hydrothermal areas with their geysers, boiling pools and mudpots. But if you choose you can follow the 150 miles of trails through the Park oblivious to its geologic history and just enjoy the scenery. Although not all routes are covered in this guide, a reference is made to most of them. If you want to create new loops or hikes refer to the free brochure that includes a map of the trail system and is available at Park entrance and ranger stations. Be reminded that an entrance fee is charged for National Parks and that dogs, and all pets for that matter, are prohibited on trails.

In 1915 the high point in the Park officially became known as Lassen Peak but until then it had been called several Indian names (all of which acknowledged its fiery origins), San Jose, Mt. Joseph, Mt. St. Joseph, Lassens Butte and Mt. Lassen. Peter Lassen was born in 1800 in Denmark and after stays in Boston and Oregon City acquired in the early '40's a 22,000 acre ranch in the Sacramento Valley where he sheltered many travelers, including Lt. John Fremont. He went to Missouri to bring settlers back along his route that went east of the present Park, an alignment that was soon replaced by William Nobles' superior one (see No. 11). Lassen lost title to the ranch, moved to Honey Lake where he and 19 others set up the territory of Nataqua, which later became the territory of Nevada, and was murdered there in 1859.

Trips in the area outside the Park not described here include hikes in the Thousand Lakes Wilderness just northwest of the Park in the Lassen National Forest. Two recommended routes there include the ones to Lake Eiler and Magee Peak. For here, and all areas managed by the US Forest Service, you're encouraged to purchase a recreation map. They provide an overview of the entire forest, or Wilderness if one exists, and show trails and other features you might want to investigate.

The three trails in the Lakes Basin Recreation Area (No's. 21, 22 and 23) are absolutely delightful—the region is like a miniature High Sierra. The fishing is purported to be as excellent as the scenery. Although Sierra Buttes (No. 24) actually is some 40 miles from the northern end of the Sierra, its dramatic and highly visible presence makes it the gateway to the range. In many ways the Grouse Lakes area, the most westerly section in the Sierra portion of this book, is like the Gold Lakes region in that it is compressed and complex. Several other trails in addition to the two described here (No's. 25 and 26) criss-cross the

Grouse Lakes area, so it's another one where a recreation map is recommended. No's. 28 and 29 head north and south, respectively, from Donner Pass and No's. 30 and 31 start from Squaw Valley and near the adjacent Alpine Meadows Ski Area. Mt. Rose (No. 32) is the most easterly and highest point in this guide. As the introduction to the hike emphasizes, the climb is considerably more scenic than you'd expect and the view is as spectacular as you'd assume. Among the impressive number of sights you'll see from the top is a perspective of the faulting that formed the Lake Tahoe Basin. The Carson Range, of which Mt. Rose is a part, rose along a boundary fault on the east side and the mountains to the west, of which Mt. Tallac (No. 35) is the high point, rose along the fault on that side and the area in between slowly and unevenly settled and was filled with a lake. Trips No's. 33 through 45 traverse the Desolation Wilderness and that area didn't become such a popular preserve for nothing. Here the glaciers that covered the entire area, with the exception of a few of the highest peaks, did their most artistic work. The somewhat less impressive—and also less traveled —trails in the northern portion are not covered in this guide but you could combine the routes described here with ones on the Forest Service's wilderness recreation map. Two (No's. 49 and 50) of the final four trails are in the Mokelumne Wilderness south of Carson Pass.

Hikers, if they were so inclined, could do almost all of the Pacific Crest Trail through Oregon and a large portion of it through Washington as day hikes. In California not only are the individual sections not so easily accessible but many portions of the PCT do not travel through prime terrain, particularly in the Lassen Peak area. There the trail is between the good stuff to the west and east. You'll be on the PCT for short distances on hikes No's 3, 4, 24, 28, 34 and 50 and for long distances on No's. 29, 30, 31, 36, 37, 38 and 48. You'll also be on the Tahoe-Yosemite Trail for all of No's. 33, 48 and 50 and the sections that concurrently follow the alignment of the PCT from Velma Lakes south to Carson Pass.

Keep in mind that once you leave freeways and main roads travel is going to be slower. Access to most of the trailheads is over paved roads. The exceptions are the hikes in Lassen Volcanic National Park not off California 89 (No's. 11, 12, 13, 14, 17, 18, 19 and 20), the two in the Caribou Wilderness (No's. 15 and 16), the two in the Grouse Lakes area (No's. 25 and 26) and those out of Wrights Lake (No's. 41 through 45).

Unfortunately, or fortunately depending on your views, all trails except those in Wilderness areas and Lassen Volcanic National Park are open to mountain bicycles. The people at the Park have put obvious signs at each trailhead indicating that ATBs (all terrain bicycles) are prohibited. The Forest Service, to date, does so only sporadically and these few signs usually are handwritten notes. Although citations are issued by some districts, such as the ones in charge of the Mokelumne Wilderness, hikers and backpackers will find illegal tire tracks on many wilderness trails.

hiking in the Lassen-Tahoe Area

BACKPACKERS WILL NEED WILDERNESS OR CAMPFIRE PERMITS FOR EVERY TRIP IN THIS GUIDE. Quotas for backpackers exist in the Desolation Wilderness. If you're planning a trip there and know the dates and the itinerary well ahead of time you can obtain a permit by mail. However, be informed that only a percentage are available by mail—the remainder are distributed on a first-come-first-serve basis the day, or previous day, of issuance. Permits also are required for most day hikes on trails under the jurisdiction of the Lake Tahoe Basin Management Unit and for the other four trails (No's. 41 through 45) in the Desolation Wilderness. Mention is made in the capsule for each specific trip if day hiking permits are required. During the summer, a Visitor Information Center is in operation at the south end of Lake Tahoe. The phone number is (916) 573-2674. The entrance road heads north from California 89 3.1 miles west of its junction with US 50 at South Lake Tahoe. The spur to the Center is about 0.1 mile west of the road to Fallen Leaf Lake and Campground. For trails not under the jurisdiction of the Lake Tahoe Basin Management Unit or in Lassen Volcanic National Park refer to the listing elsewhere in this guide for which trails belong to what ranger district. When you have specific questions about a hike it's going to be the district actually managing the area that will be able to answer them. The exception to this, as the agency listing shows, is that queries and permits for trails No's. 39 through 45 are answered by a central information center.

Begin each hike with adequate water and, if you're backpacking, always carry a purification system. If you're staying somewhere nearby with a freezer put a couple plastic bottles filled with water (leaving a little extra room for expansion) in it overnight. If the day isn't too warm and you don't eat too late you'll have refreshingly frigid water with lunch. Given the high number of hikers and backpackers in the Lassen—Tahoe area, not to mention the meadows that are also populated with range cattle, most of the water sources are suspect, if not absolutely guilty. However, there are a few, such as springs, or streams that come from

6

unvisited areas that probably would be safe to drink untreated. People do vary in how they react intestinally to what they eat and drink and most long-time hikers and backpackers probably have built up some resistances to many bugs. If you do opt to drink from these carefully selected sources, just be reminded that you are gambling. (Such statements are an anathema to some—even thinking about drinking untreated water is heretical.)

Since all these hikes are in mountainous terrain where the weather is capable of becoming nasty very quickly, it's always prudent to carry the essentials: wool hat, gloves, sweater, windbreaker, waterproof garment, whistle, first aid kit, map of the area, compass (if you know how to use it—and even if you don't, figuring out how might keep you occupied until you're found), flashlight and a little extra food. Even on the balmiest day someone in your party could become injured and they'll need some of that extra gear until help arrives. Also take with you all your valuables, such as wallet, keys and camera. Never leave them in your trunk or even try to hide them because beady eyes may well be watching and their owners will head right for the spot after you've left. Any purloinable items you can't carry with you, such as tape decks and cassettes, etc., should be left at home.

Although athletic shoes are fine for occasional hikes on reasonably smooth treads, a light weight boot gives much more support and is recommended for backpackers and for people hiking day after day. When rain looks likely, pack a man's large umbrella. It can keep your head, torso, glasses and the top of your pack dry and, surprisingly, is not tiring to carry. A poncho-like garment still is best for doing camp chores. Another recommended accouterment is a hiking cane. It's a welcome third leg while fording streams and traveling over rough terrain and can give relief to grumbling knees on steep downhill grades. One can even help you go uphill faster, if you're so inclined. If you can't find any in your local outdoor store, try a surgical supply outlet. Buy a model with a curved handle so you can hook it over your arm when you need both hands free.

Along the trails in this guide you'll be traveling at moderately high elevations and frequently in the open. Most people shouldn't have much trouble with the altitude. Just take a slower pace if your body is being recalcitrant. If you're getting headaches, make a conscious effort to breathe more deeply, particularly on the downhill sections, where you wouldn't be doing so automatically. Wear a sunblock, hat and sunglasses on all but the most wooded hikes. People who are very sun sensitive and will be backpacking or hiking day after day might want to wear a sleeved shirt and cotton gloves. Although these suggestions about breathing and sun protection are more pertinent to the higher, more open areas of the Sierra to the south, some people may find them useful for the Lassen and Tahoe areas as well.

Lightning storms are not uncommon. When you realize a thunderstorm is building (and after you've been caught in a couple you'll know very well what the signs are), immediately retreat from summits and exposed ridges into deep timber—don't huddle under a lone tree or a small grove. With the exception of Lassen Peak and a few other hikes in this guide you're fortunately never far from timberline.

Stream crossings shouldn't be a problem, even early in the season, for any hikes in this guide. However, if you have any suspicions about the safety of a ford anywhere, don't try it. Normally, you won't even get your boots more than superficially wet crossing the streams on the trails in this book but when you do come to a ford that is safe but still deep enough that you know you're going to get your feet wet you have three options in addition to simply stomping across with both boots and socks on (going across barefoot is not one of them—the odds are high that you'll cut or bruise your feet): first and best is to carry a pair of tennis shoes to change into for the ford so both your boots and socks stay dry. If you're backpacking, you'll most likely have the tennies along for camp wear anyway. Secondly, you can take off your boots, wade across in your socks and then thoroughly wring them out on the other side before putting your boots back on. Thirdly, take off your socks and wear the boots across.

Backcountry visitors in California tend to mind their outdoor manners. A tidy bunch, overall, but it's gracious to pick-up and pack-out the bits of debris that have been left by others. Keep in mind that egg shells and orange rinds are two kinds of organic matter that decompose slowly so put them back in your lunch sack. If you defecate, do so well away from the trail and at least 200 feet from streams and lakes. Pretend you're a cat by first digging a hole and then afterwards returning the top soil and gently tamping it down. Women should carry a little plastic bag in which to put personal hygiene items and then dispose of them at home.

NEVER SHORTCUT SWITCHBACKS. It can be dangerous to those below but the primary reason for the prohibition is that doing so results in unsightly erosion channels. Nature does quite enough destruction without help from humans. If you come to sections of trail where lingering snow covers the tread, try to stay on the alignment. Detouring around snow may be easier at the time but it scars the adjacent terrain, which will no doubt be fragile from being moist. Another prohibition is not to pick any wildflowers—

leave them for others to enjoy. Aural — as well as visual — pollution, such as shouting, radios and barking dogs and so on, doesn't belong in the outdoors.

Backpackers, because of their greater impact, have to be even more aware of their actions. The Golden Rule for them, as well as hikers, is "Be inconspicuous". In other words, there should be no evidence you were ever there. Don't make any permanent changes in the camp area, such as hip holes or tent trenches. Not only are primus type stoves preferable, in many areas they are required and wood fires prohibited. More subtle aspects of No Trace Camping are the scattering of a few cones and other appropriate debris over your camp area just before you leave so it appears more natural and buying earth toned, rather than vividly hued, clothing and equipment that blends in with the landscape. Brochures on proper hiking and backpacking techniques are available at ranger stations and visitor centers and you're encouraged to read them.

When you have questions, suggestions, complaints or compliments on how the trails and terrain are being managed write to the appropriate agency. The addresses for Lassen Volcanic National Park and the relevant National Forests and their ranger districts are listed in this guide. Your input is important. On matters concerning a National Forest, send copies to both the regional office and the appropriate ranger district(s), if applicable. Comments for the authors can be sent to them in care of The Touchstone Press, P.O. Box 81, Beaverton, Oregon 97075. All the trails in this guide were hiked by the Lowes but keep in mind that conditions can change from natural causes, such as landslides, or, in the case of such things as permits, from policy decisions.

Good Hiking!

D.L.
R.L.

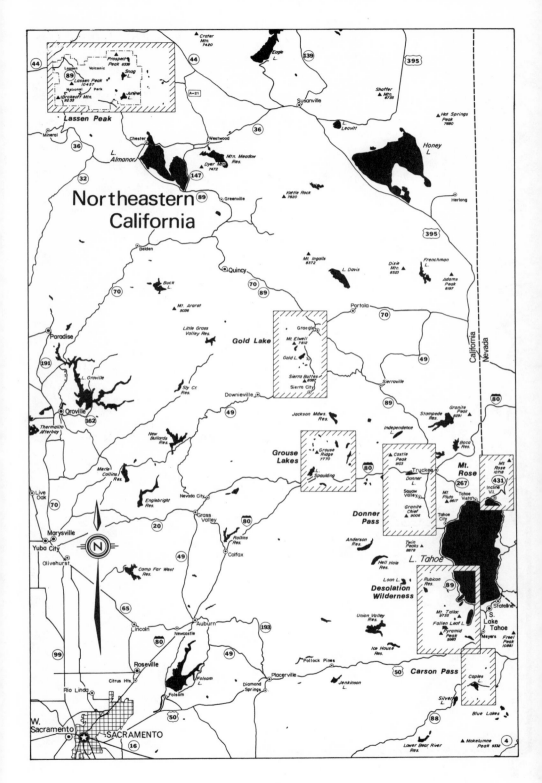

Northeastern California

LEGEND

Trail Head	●
Trail	- - - -
Campsite	△
Mileage	5.6
Trail No.	No. 6E03
Highway No.	(80)
Primary Road	▬
Secondary Road	= = = =

agency listings

Listed below are the addresses and phone numbers for the government agencies having jurisdiction over the trails described in this guide. The relevant hike numbers are shown for each agency.

Lassen Volcanic National Park Mineral, California 96063 (916) 595-4444	1, 2, 3, 4, 5, 6, 7, 8, 9, 10, 11, 12, 13, 14, 17, 18, 19, 20
Almanor Ranger District Lassen National Forest P.O. Box 767 Chester, California 96020 (916) 258-2141	15, 16
Beckworth Ranger District Plumas National Forest P.O. Box 7 Blairsden, California 96105 (916) 836-2575	21, 22, 23
Tahoe National Forest Highway 49 and Coyote Street Nevada City, California 95959 (916) 265-4531	
Downieville Ranger District 15924 Highway 49 Camptonville, California 95922-9707 (916) 288-3231	24
Nevada City Ranger District Highway 49 and Coyote Street Nevada City, California 95959 (916) 265-4538	25, 26, 27
Truckee Ranger District P.O. Box 399 Truckee, California 95734 (916) 587-3558	28, 29, 30, 31
Lake Tahoe Basin Management Unit 870 Emerald Bay Road (Calif. 89) P.O. Box 8465 South Lake Tahoe, California 95731 (916) 573-2600	32, 33, 34, 35, 36, 37, 38, 46 48 (north of Meiss Pass)
Visitor Information Center (summer only) 3.1 miles west of junction of US 50 and Califorina 89 at South Lake Tahoe Open weekends only from 10 a.m. to 4 p.m. Memorial Day through the end of June and from after Labor Day through Nov. 1 Open 7 days a week from 8 a.m. to 6 p.m. from the end of June through Labor Day (916) 573-2674	
Eldorado National Forest 100 Forni Road Placerville, California 95667 (916) 622-5061	
Hiker and Backpacker Information 3070 Camino Heights Drive Camino, California 95709 (916) 644-6048	39, 40, 41, 42, 43, 44, 45
Amador Ranger District 26820 Silver Drive Pioneer, California 95666 (209) 295-4251	47, 48 (to Meiss Pass), 49, 50

contents

Lassen Peak from Kings Creek Meadow

area map–lassen par

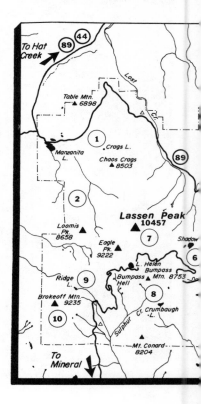

14

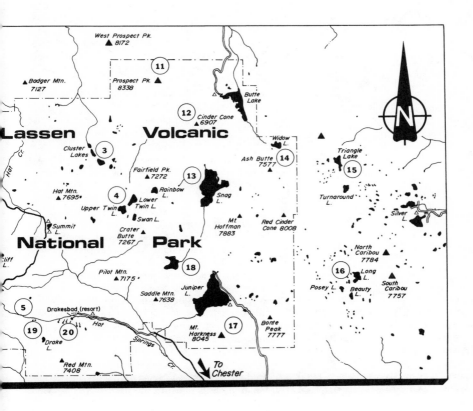

West Prospect Pk.
▲ 8172

⑪

▲ Badger Mtn.
7127

Prospect Pk. ▲
8338

Butte
Lake

Lassen

⑫ Cinder Cone
▲ 6907

Volcanic

Widow
L.

Cluster
Lakes ③

Fairfield Pk.
▲ 7272 ⑬

Ash Butte ⑭
7577

Triangle
Lake

Hat Mtn.
▲ 7695•

④

Rainbow
L.

Lower
Twin L.

Snag
L.

⑮

Turnaround
L.

Upper Twin L.

Silver
L.

Swan L.

Mt.
Hoffman
7883

Red Cinder
Cone 8008

Summit
L.

Crater
Butte ▲
7267

National

Park

North
Caribou ▲
7784

Cliff
L.

Pilot Mtn.
▲ 7175

⑱

⑯ Long
L.

Posey L.

Beauty
L.

South
Caribou ▲
7757

Saddle Mtn.
▲ 7638

Juniper
L.

⑤

Drakesbad (resort)

Hot

Bonte
Peak
7777

⑲

⑳

Mt.
Harkness ▲
8045

⑰

Drake
L.

Springs

Red Mtn.
7408

▲ To
Chester

N

1 CHAOS CRATER

One day trip
Distance: 2 miles one way
Elevation gain: 800 feet; loss 100 feet
High point: 6,700 feet
Allow 1 to 1¼ hours one way
Usually open mid June through mid
**   October**
Topographic map:
** U.S.G.S. Manzanita Lake, Calif.**
** 15'   1956**

Geologists are especially taken with the Chaos Crags just north of Lassen Peak because, among other reasons, this formation is so young. One source states they may have risen around 1700 A.D.—people reported that the rocks were constantly emitting steam and gases in the mid-1850's. Other scientists write the Crags may be as much as 1,200 years old but, in any case, they are not aged. Chaos Crags is a plug dome like Lassen Peak, only smaller and younger. Plug domes are formed when the lava forced out of a vent is so thick it is pushed upward rather than flowing outward. The crater at the destination of this hike was created by violent blasts of steam. The extent of the immense rockslide, called Chaos Jumbles, that resulted from the undermining of that area of the Crags can be studied along the final section of the trip. One portion of this slide blocked Manzanita Creek, thus forming Manzanita Lake. Snag Lake (No. 13) also was created by the blockage of a creek but it was from a more conventional lava flow. The second to the last explanation of how a rockslide like the Jumbles could cover such a vast area was that the debris rode an air cushion. The latest theory, buttressed by lunar photographs showing similar slides, is that the rocks remain airborne a bit longer because they maintain momentum from colliding off each other.

Early in the season Crags Lake, the destination of this hike, fills the crater but usually it has done a disappearing act by late summer. Even though the trail is through a variety of woods until just before the lake (or the crater, depending on when you visit), the relatively low elevation can make it warmer than the average Lassen area hike. So, if you have a choice save it for a cooler day.

From the Manzanita Lake entrance proceed southeast on California 89 past the lake to a sign marking the road south to a campground and store. Turn onto this spur and after about 200 yards come to a sign on the left identifying the beginning of the Chaos Crags Trail.

Walk on the level among widely spaced big pines across volcanic ash. On your left and around the trailhead area used to be a store, lodge, museum and cabins. However, because of the batholith that still lurks under the area and the avalanches that could result from renewed activity, Park Service personnel decided to remove the buildings. Begin climbing on a firmer tread and then descend in deeper woods, cross a creek and pass a spring. Travel on the level and then begin a gentle climb. As you gain elevation the woods again become more open and your nose will be treated to the pleasingly astringent scent characteristic of pine forests.

Near 0.9 mile have a set of short, but steep, switchbacks and continue up at a grade less than the switchbacks but greater than before the turns. After about another 0.5 mile switch back right and then curve left. Have a short down and then resume rising through open woods of sturdy pines with a manzanita ground cover. Abruptly, the bushes stop and are replaced by small rocks. Come to the crest of the ridge where you can look down into the crater holding the lake. A rough trail goes the several hundred yards down to the floor of the bowl.

Crags Lake

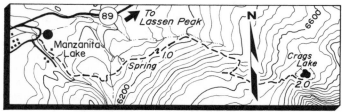

2 MANZANITA CREEK

One day trip
Distance: 5 miles one way
Elevation gain: 1,700 feet
High point: 7,550 feet
Allow 3½ to 4½ hours one way
Usually open late June through mid
October
Topographic maps:
  U.S.G.S. Lassen Peak, Calif.
  15'   1956
  U.S.G.S. Manzanita Lake, Calif.
  15'   1956

The 4.0 mile long route that heads south from near Manzanita Lake and eventually parallels Manzanita Creek originally was a fire road but today serves as a hiking trail. It meanders up mostly through woods of widely spaced trees to a verdant clearing that is a boisterous flower garden during the blooming season. This is a satisfying place to end the trip and would lessen the elevation gain listed in the capsule by 400 feet. However, adventurous hikers are enthusiastically urged to continue cross-country another mile up to a valley of immense meadows on the western flank of Lassen Peak, a gorgeous, lush area unlike any other in the Park. You'll want to allow extra time to explore some of its nooks and crannies.

From the Manzanita Lake entrance station drive southeast on California 89 past the lake to the sign marking the road south to a campground and store. Follow this spur and in 200 yards pass the signed beginning of the Chaos Crags Trail (No. 1). Farther on pass the store and continue south along the road to the campground, staying straight (left) on the main road where routes head right until you come to Loop F and a sign marking the start of the Manzanita Creek Trail.

The initial several tenths mile of the road is soft volcanic ash bordered by masses of seemingly dead manzanita, victims of nothing more ominous than their natural growth cycle. The views ahead to Chaos Crags and Lassen Peak (No. 7) are compensation. Eventually, the road enters those pleasing, open woods of red fir and other conifers. After 1.6 miles of moderate, but persistent, uphill have a level stretch and, farther on, a slight drop to another level area, this one with sparse grass. Prior to the big flower show at the end of the road you'll have previews with scattered blooms of pennyroyal, penstemon, gilia, columbine and lupine.

At 2.4 miles the road crosses Manzanita Creek and continues winding up for a few tenths mile more over gentle slopes before beginning a traverse above a bush lined stretch of Manzanita Creek. Just before the end of the road come to the north end of the meadow. Cross a small side stream and continue past those promised wildflowers. Among the masses of yellow and white blooms look for the purple stalks of monkshood. Someone hurrying by could easily mistake them for larkspur, also a member of the buttercup family, but closer examination will reveal the hood from which the flower gets its common name.

To make that highly recommended cross-country extension continue through the clearing to the end of the road. Your immediate goal is at the top of the slope across the creek to the south and a bit west. However, heading directly there will take you through dense bushes and deep goo. So, turn left (east) and follow the course of least resistance. Turn south (right) as soon as you can avoid the bushes and cross some blowdown. The farther east you head before veering south the more blowdown you'll need to negotiate. If you've aimed just right you'll find yourself in a narrow corridor through the trees that leads to the stream. Hop the flow, in 50 feet or so come to the slope and begin climbing. You'll most likely meet a cross trail. Turn left and follow it up to the crest. Be sure to note landmarks beyond here so you can return along the same route—or a corrected one, if necessary. Turn right where you come to the edge of the slope and walk west before curving south into the valley. You can head toward the upper end of the huge meadow and make a counterclockwise loop back to where you met the north edge of the valley. If you have the time and inclination the slopes to the south definitely merit further cross-country explorations.

Upper Manzanita Creek Meadows

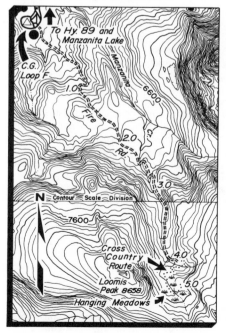

3 CLUSTER LAKES

One day trip or backpack
Distance: 4.8 miles one way
Elevation gain: 670 feet; loss 770 feet
High point: 7,320 feet
Allow 2½ hours one way
Usually open mid June through October
Topographic maps:
   U.S.G.S. Mt. Harkness, Calif.
   15′   1956
   U.S.G.S. Prospect Peak, Calif.
   15′   1957

Given the choice, almost all hikers and backpackers would prefer to travel under dry skies but they know gloom and rain occasionally will be their companions. So it's the prudent hiker who has a reserve list of routes that lose little by being done in cloudy or wet conditions. One of these in the Lassen area is the trip from Summit Lake to the Cluster Lakes because when the visibility is low there are no far-ranging views to miss, with the exception of one to Lassen Peak (No. 7) and Chaos Crags (No. 1) near the 0.5 mile point. However, the close-in scenery is interesting with its variety of woods and seven lakes. Of course, clear skies don't diminish this—or any—outing. With just 2.0 miles of additional hiking you could make a loop by returning along the trail to Upper and Lower Twin Lakes (No. 4).

Proceed on California 89 for 11.9 miles south of the Manzanita Lake entrance or 16.6 miles north of the southwest entrance to North Summit Lake Campground. Follow the road into the campground

and park in turnouts on the right a few hundred feet from the highway.

Walk along the campground road, paralleling the lake and staying right (straight) where loops head left. At a sign on your right pointing to Amphitheater turn onto the path and walk near the northeast shore of Summit Lake for 150 yards to a fork and a sign with many mileages. The trail to the right continues to South Summit Lake Campground. Turn left and begin an 0.8 mile climb that starts at a gradual grade but increases a bit farther on. Come to a crest and travel on the level to a fork. If you make the suggested loop, you'll be returning along the route to the right.

Stay left, follow a levelish, meandering course and then climb to another crest. Begin descending and pass an unnamed lake. Climb above it and have a series of short up and down stretches through more rugged terrain. Descend to Little Bear Lake and continue down briefly to Big Bear Lake. As you've headed northeast and downhill the forest has gradually changed from one of large, widely spaced trees to more abundant, smaller ones with no manzanita ground cover. With its tangle of red branches and masses of soft green, little leaves, manzanita certainly is an attractive plant but it is usually associated with more open, drier slopes so woods without it often seem cooler and deeper. A member of the heath family, there are around 40 species of manzanita in California. Continue gradually down to a T-junction. You can turn left to visit the two most northerly components of the Cluster Lake chain. The trail continues north for 2.0 miles to the Pacific Crest Trail.

To visit Silver and Feather Lakes or make the suggested loop, turn right. Walk on the level to Silver Lake and then have a wee climb and drop to Feather Lake, the only member of the chain where campsites are not abundant.

To make the loop continue along the trail from Feather Lake and pass a pond on your left and then one on your right. Have some short, but never steep, uphill sections cross a stream bed, which most likely will be dry, and climb briefly to an old road that is identified as the Emigrant Trail (see No. 11). From here to Twin Lakes you'll also be walking along a section of the PCT. Unfortunately people doing the PCT who don't have time to explore the terrain away from it will miss the best of Lassen Park because of the route's easterly alignment.

Turn right, after 0.2 mile pass a ranger cabin on your left and come to a meadowy strip extending beyond the north end of Lower Twin Lake. The northwest side provides some of the best swimming. Trails follow both the west and east shorelines but the shortest way to the other end and the continuation of the loop is along the west side.

Lassen Peak from Summit Lake

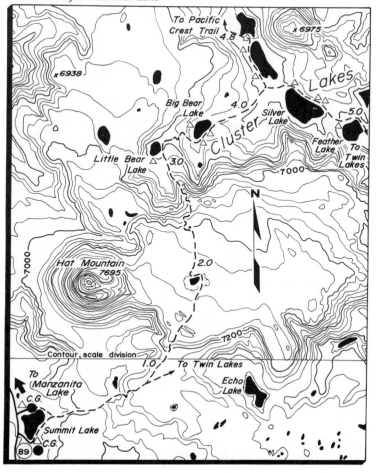

4 UPPER and LOWER TWIN LAKES

One day trip or backpack
Distance: 4 miles one way
Elevation gain: 510 feet; loss 620 feet
High point: 7,160 feet
Allow 2 hours one way
Usually open mid June through October
Topographic maps:
  U.S.G.S. Mt. Harkness, Calif.
  15'   1956
  U.S.G.S. Prospect Peak, Calif.
  15'   1957

Unlike the trips to such grand landmarks as Lassen Peak (No. 7) or Brokeoff Mountain (No. 10) where hikers are reminded of their insignificance in the big scheme of things or to the hydrothermal areas (No's. 8, 9, 19 and 20) where they ponder what was going on even before their primordial origins, the trail to Upper and Lower Twin Lakes leads travelers through charming, human scaled terrain. As is common in the Lassen area, the route passes a variety of vegetation, even though the elevation change is not great. Lower Twin Lake makes for particularly good swimming but on a really warm day you might want to splash around in Upper Twin Lake, Echo Lake and a large pond that you also visit. You can make a loop by combining this trail to Upper and Lower Twin Lakes with the one to Cluster Lakes (No. 3). Most people would agree that the scenery along the Twin Lakes Trail is more attractive so which leg you do first depends on whether you want

the better sooner or later.

Backpackers could establish a base camp at Lower Twin Lake and make day hikes to the east, south and north. One recommended itinerary would be the loop that passes Horsehoe (No. 18), Snag (No. 13) and Rainbow Lakes.

Drive on California 89 for 11.9 miles south of the Manzanita Lake entrance or 16.6 miles north of the southwest entrance to the road to North Summit Lake Campground. Follow the spur into the campground and park in turnouts on the right a few hundred feet from the highway.

Walk along the road, paralleling the lake and staying right (straight) where loops head left. At a sign on your right pointing to Amphitheater turn onto the path and walk near the northeast shore of Summit Lake for 150 yards to a fork and a sign with many mileages. The trail to the right continues to South Summit Lake Campground. Turn left and begin an 0.8 mile climb that starts at a gradual grade but increases a bit farther on. About half way up turn around for a view of Chaos Crags (No. 1) and Lassen Peak (No. 7). Come to a crest and travel on the level to a fork. The trail to the left goes to the Cluster Lakes.

Stay right and climb gently through woods of big, widely spaced trees with clumps of manzanita ground cover. Begin descending and traverse down a slope of dense manzanita and other bushes. Reenter deeper woods and continue down to Echo Lake. The trail turns left, curves right and then travels along its northeast shore. Note that camping is not permitted here.

Climb briefly and then begin descending. Pass a little pond on your right, have some more downhill and then walk at a level or very gradual grade to a long, narrow pond. Travel beside then above it and beyond the east end wind down to Upper Twin Lake. Stay left, follow the attractively wooded north shore and then descend through a little canyon to Lower Twin Lake. Trails go along both the east and west sides so, if you're not doing the big loop past Cluster Lakes, you can make a circuit around Lower Twin Lake. On the east side you'll be following the Pacific Crest Trail. Some of the best swimming is at the northwest end of Lower Twin Lake.

If you're making the big loop you'll most likely opt to follow the trail along the west side of Lower Twin Lake to its north end. From there continue north on the narrow old road. This is a portion of the Emigrant Trail (see No. 11) and you'll also be on the PCT along this stretch. Soon pass a ranger cabin on your right and 0.4 mile from the lake come to a signed junction, turn left and follow the trail for another 1.0 mile to Feather Lake, the most easterly of the Cluster Lakes.

Scene at Lower Twin Lake

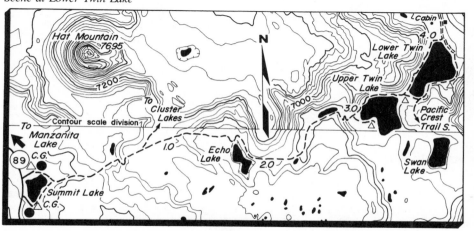

5 SIFFORD LAKES

One day trip
Distance: 2.6 miles one way
Elevation gain: 400 feet; loss 500 feet
High point: 7,280 feet
Allow 1½ hours one way
Usually open July through October
Topographic map:
   U.S.G.S. Mt. Harkness, Calif.
   15'   1956

The hike to the Sifford Lakes travels through a portion of the immense, lush meadow bordering Kings Creek, with the possible exception of Drakesbad Meadow (No's. 19 and 20) the most impressive clearing in the Park. The hike also traverses a narrow, rocky gorge past the Cascades to Kings Creek Falls, two cataracts that would be noteworthy anywhere. The remainder of the route meanders through a remarkable variety of woods to the chain of lakes, the first of which makes for good swimming. You're encouraged to do the trip as a loop that affords new scenery plus saves a bit of distance and 400 feet of uphill.

Proceed on California 89 for 16.7 miles south of the Manzanita Lake entrance or 11.8 miles north of the southwest entrance to a sign stating Kings Creek Elevation 7,250, a 32 Marker and space for parking all off the south shoulder. There may be no actual trail sign here.

From the south side of the highway hike downhill to verdant Lower Meadow and walk on the level to a junction. The possible loop returns along the trail to your right. Stay left, following the sign to Kings Creek Cascade and Falls, have a little climb and then farther on stay right at the junction of the horse trail that bypasses the Cascade. After a short distance begin descending the stone steps along the wall of the gorge holding the Cascade. Near the bottom of the little canyon resume traveling on a dirt tread. Stay right where the horse trail rejoins and continue down an increasingly gentle grade to the junction of the spur to a view of Kings Creek Falls, whose basic stairstep configuration is ornamented with nubbins of rocks, creating a plethora of routes for the water to follow.

After returning from the view of the falls cross Kings Creek on a footlog and climb moderately in woods to near the base of a scarp. Parallel the length of the long rock wall, climb, level off and then descend past a ground cover of manzanita to Bench Lake.

You can descend along the trail to the junction of the route to Drakesbad, turn right and climb back up to the spur to Sifford Lakes. However, a better way for people who are comfortable with cross-country travel is to leave the trail just past Bench Lake and parallel its east shore. Beyond the lake continue south, keeping a rock wall on your right. Bear slightly left and soon be looking for a meadowy area off on the left. Walk its length to near the southeast end of the clearing to a cross trail, the one you'll be following back if you make the recommended loop. Most likely, you'll be a bit above (to the west) of the signed spur to Sifford Lakes so you'll need to turn left.

From the junction of the spur to Sifford Lakes descend across an exceptionally attractive slope of manzanita and widely spaced trees for 0.1 mile, climb for 0.2 mile and abruptly come to the lowest and largest of the chain. Turn left and follow the trail around to the west end. The terrain south of the lake is good for some short off trail exploring.

If you want to continue to the next higher lake, follow the path up to the northwest from the west end of the lake. The route isn't obvious near the shoreline but after a short distance it's no problem to follow. From the second lake veer to the right and climb past a couple of smaller ones. Experienced hikers can continue up due north and then descend over gentle terrain to the junction with the return loop.

The return circuit climbs moderately through woods unlike any enjoyed earlier and then begins a gentle descent to Lower Meadow. Cross a stream on a log, in a few hundred feet meet the trail you took in and turn left.

Kings Creek

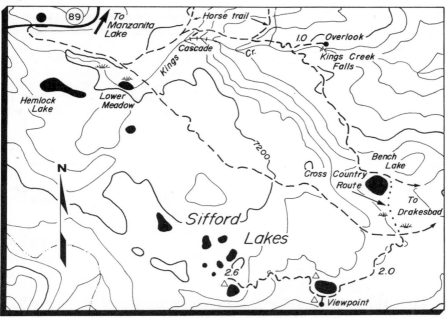

6   SHADOW and CLIFF LAKES

One day trip
Distance: 1.7 miles one way
Elevation loss: 700 feet
High point: 8,050 feet
Allow ¾ to 1 hour one way
Usually open July through October
Topographic map:
  U.S.G.S. Mt. Harkness, Calif.
  15′   1956

zones. With its hydrothermal areas, several kinds of volcanic mountains and remnants and many lakes, Lassen Volcanic National Park has considerably more variety that would result solely from a low point of 5,250 feet in Warner Valley to 10,457 foot Lassen Peak (No. 7). The prime timberline zone in the Park surrounds the Helen Lake area just south of Lassen Peak. The first mile of the trail to Bumpass Hell (No. 8) travels through this area and the route down past Terrace, Shadow and Cliff Lakes begins near timberline and descends into the next vegetation zone of meadows and deeper woods. As with Park features as a whole, these three lakes are each in completely different settings, despite the short distances separating them.

A trail continues northeast from the Cliff Lake junction to California 89 at Summit Lake so you could establish a car shuttle. A trail also heads north from the 0.2 mile point to Hat Lake off 89 so you have the opportunity for another one way hike. Camping is not permitted at any of the three lakes passed on this hike.

Drive on California 89 for 19.5 miles south of the Manzanita Lake entrance or 9.0 miles north of the southwest entrance to the 27 Marker. (This is 2.0 miles east of the large parking area for the Lassen Peak Trail.)

Descend through open, boulder dotted woods for 0.2 mile to the junction of the trail that travels down for 2.2 miles through Paradise Meadow to Hat Lake at California 89. Keep right, continue descending through subalpine woods and farther on you can see ahead down to Terrace Lake. Switch back once to the bench holding the lake and walk along its south shore.

From the little rim just beyond Terrace Lake have a view of Shadow Lake, the largest of the three you'll be visiting. It's the most open—not in woods like Terrace nor bordered by a high rock wall like Cliff. Travel at the water's edge along the southeast shore. On a warm day later in the summer you could have a nice swim here. Beyond the east end resume descending and then travel through a small basin filled with grass, ponds and scattered trees. Have a wee climb and then hike downhill in woods to the junction of the spur to Cliff Lake. The route to the left is the one that continues down for 1.8 miles to Summit Lake.

Turn right, drop through a forest of close growing smaller trees and no ground cover and then travel beside the pretty, grass rimmed outlet stream just before coming to Cliff Lake.

Although it will be uphill all the way back, you will have many sightings of Lassen Peak looming ahead during the climb.

Almost any area with considerable relief will have varied scenery if for no other reason than the changes in elevation support different vegetation

Cliff Lake

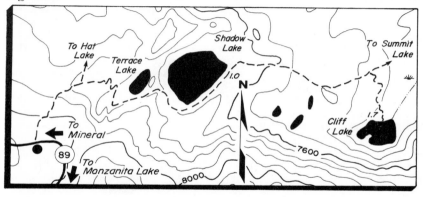

7   LASSEN PEAK

One day trip
Distance: 2.2 miles one way
Elevation gain: 2,000 feet
High point: 10,457 feet
Allow 2 hours one way
Usually open July through October
Topographic map:
  U.S.G.S. Lassen Peak, Calif.
  15′   1956

Few mountains 10,500 feet high have excellent trails—or even rustic paths—to their summits but Lassen Peak does. It is the highest point in Lassen Volcanic National Park and also the most southerly major landmark in the Cascade Range, that chain of mountains extending through Oregon and Washington into Canada. The views during the climb and from the summit extend, not surprisingly, over the Park to far distant features.

Because you'll be in the open and at high elevations for the entire hike, you should wear sunglasses and a hat and use a sunblock on exposed skin, including arms and legs. Begin with adequate water and also carry extra clothing in case the summit area is windy or cold. Camping is not allowed along the trail or on the summit. As with any hike to peaks or along exposed ridges, don't begin or continue if a storm is brewing.

Proceed on California 89 for 21.5 miles south of the Manzanita Lake entrance or 7.0 miles north of the southwest entrance to the 22 Marker where there is an immense parking area.

Acquire one of the informative brochures about Lassen Peak available at the trailhead. Along this hike you'll be having continual close-up looks at a volcano that was spectacularly active as recently as 1915. Traverse up an open slope, switch back and enter a grove of tall trees, the first and last shade along the climb. Cross a basin and travel above a portable outhouse. One also is located at 1.5 miles before the final series of switchbacks to the crater rim. Walk by a section of dense lupine. Like that finger of woods, they are the only masses of wildflowers you'll encounter along the hike. However, as you continue up you won't be disappointed by the lack of abundant vegetation but instead delighted and amazed at the few hardy examples you do see. You'll also be impressed with the apparently robust ground squirrels scurrying over the slopes near the top.

The technique for climbing at high elevations (or on soft surfaces like sand dunes and volcanic ash) is to maintain a steady, relatively slow pace. If you have to stop frequently, you're going too fast. Soon you'll be able to see Brokeoff Mountain (No. 10) and Lake Almanor to the south. As you continue switch backing you'll have views down onto Helen Lake and then to Prospect Peak (No. 11), Cinder Cone (No. 12) and Fantastic Lava Beds in the northeast corner of the Park, to Mt. Harkness (No. 17) in the southeast and directly down to Shadow and Cliff Lakes (No. 6). NEVER SHORTCUT SWITCHBACKS. Doing so causes unsightly erosion channels and could be dangerous to people hiking below. The mileage markers you pass indicate how far you have to hike. Climb along the ridge, alternating between crossing from one side to the other and traveling on the crest.

Pass the last of the gnarled white bark pines just before the 1 mile marker. Farther on begin a longer traverse across the right (east) side of the ridge and then switch back and pass above the second outhouse. Make the final 13 switchbacks to the crater rim, remembering to STAY ON THE TRAIL. On the return the view down onto people winding up and down this section will resemble an Escher drawing.

If you want to go to the absolute summit, follow the path along the ridge forming the east rim of the crater, traverse the west slope of the summit block and then climb along the north side to the top. To explore the crater area, head north, traveling parallel to but below the summit block, to the north rim where you'll have a view over the terrain between here and Mt. Shasta.

Hikers on Summit of Lassen Peak

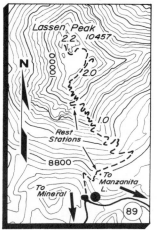

8 BUMPASS HELL – CRUMBAUGH LAKE

One day trip
Distance: 1.2 miles to Bumpass Hell;
2.6 miles additional to
Crumbaugh Lake
Elevation gain: 350 feet; loss 200 feet to
Bumpass Hell; 75 feet
gain and 1,000 feet loss
additional to Crumbaugh
Lake
High point: 8,400 feet
Allow 45 minutes to Bumpass Hell;
1½ hours additional to Crumbaugh
Lake
Usually open July through October
Topographic maps:
U.S.G.S. Lassen Peak, Calif.
15′   1956
U.S.G.S. Mt. Harkness, Calif.
15′   1956

Bumpass Hell is Lassen Volcanic National Park's convention center for thermal activity with all the hissing, steaming, bubbling and blurping going on in one 16 acre room. Boardwalks take you close to the steam vents, boiling pools and mudpots and you'll also have several overviews of the basin. The trail to it travels through some of the most attractive alpine scenery in the Park.

The route that continues beyond Bumpass Hell to Cold Boiling and Crumbaugh Lakes traverses imposing tree and wildflower covered slopes. Note that this extension is mostly downhill and that a short trail connects Cold Boiling Lake with the Kings Creek Meadows picnic area. However, this does enable you to establish a car shuttle. Another trail continues west from Crumbaugh Lake for 3.0 miles to California 89 north of the southwest entrance station so you also could set up a shuttle here. Begin with adequate water. No camping is allowed at Cold Boiling or Crumbaugh Lakes or Bumpass Hell.

Drive on California 89 for 22.3 miles south of the Manzanita Lake entrance or 6.2 miles north of the southwest entrance to the 17 and 18 Markers and a large parking area off the south side of the road. Be sure to acquire one of the excellent descriptive brochures for the Bumpass Hell Nature Trail.

Have a short downhill, passing near Helen Lake, and then begin traversing moderately uphill along the massive wall that forms the head of Little Hot Springs Valley. You can see Brokeoff Mountain (No. 10) to the southwest and back to Lassen Peak (No. 7). Where the slope on your left becomes less steep look for conies, those adorable little rodents with the squeaky bleats. Travel by an area of dense lupine and then pass a portable outhouse at a notch on your left. Continue through the exquisite alpine scene of rocks and trees to the first overlook of Bumpass Hell.

Stay right where a steeper trail comes up on the left, the top end of a little loop past Bumpass Hell that you're encouraged to follow up on the return. Traverse down, switch back once and at the far end of a bridge come to a fork. The branch to the left heads past an overlook and more thermal activity, including an exceptionally mesmerizing mudpot, and then loops back up to the main trail. Unless you're doing the hike one way only, save this left branch until the return and for now turn right and soon come to a descriptive marker for Bumpass Hell. STAY ON THE BOARDWALKS AND TRAILS AS YOU EXPLORE THE THERMAL AREA.

To continue to Crumbaugh Lake cross the bridge near the marker and at its east end pass a mileage sign. Walk along the edge of Bumpass Hell and then climb to a last overlook. Make a gentle curve across a barren area and then begin descending along wooded slopes. You can see Lake Almanor far below to the southeast and after you've curved to the northeast you'll have views down onto the lush valley holding Crumbaugh Lake and, farther on, glimpses of Cold Boiling Lake near the head of the valley.

Continue descending, crossing several streams and flower and fern packed clearings separated by fingers of woods. Curve down above the north side of Cold Boiling Lake and then walk near the east shore, passing a sign marking the gas bubblings for which it is named. Just beyond the lake come to the trail to the parking area at Kings Creek Meadows picnic area.

Stay right and continue mostly downhill in woods to a sign identifying Crumbaugh Lake. You can explore around the lake but the main route goes right. Cross a couple of inlet streams and travel through a huge open area of false hellebore, wyethia, lupine, asters and others wildflowers. To reach the north shore you'll need to leave the trail, which eventually travels near the west side and then heads down to the highway.

Bumpass Hell

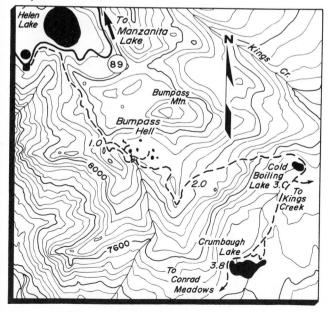

9 RIDGE LAKE

One day trip
Distance: 1 mile one way
Elevation gain: 1,000 feet
High point: 7,960 feet
Allow 1 hour one way
Usually open July through October
Topographic map:
  U.S.G.S. Lassen Peak, Calif.
  15′   1956

The hike up to Ridge Lake is a second cousin to the one to Ropi Lake (No. 40) in the Tahoe area for being an example that elevation gain, as much as distance, is important in determining how strenuous an outing will be. Although hardly as demanding as the Ropi Lake ascent, the trip to Ridge Lake is more difficult than its mile length would suggest because of the 1,000 feet of steep uphill. In addition to being a muscle stretcher, the trail also provides a great variety of high grade scenery. The route begins at the fumaroles of the Sulphur Works and after passing a viewpoint down onto a portion of the hissing and steaming vents winds up through stately woods and across good sized, flower filled meadows. People wanting even more uphill can explore the ridges above the lake that provide great views to the west and down onto Brokeoff Meadows.

Proceed on California 89 for 27.4 miles south from the Manzanita Lake entrance or 1.1 miles north from the southwest entrance to the parking area at Sulphur Works. A sign at the north side of the parking area identifies the beginning of the trail to Ridge Lake.

After several yards curve right, have those views onto a portion of the hydrothermal area and then travel up a little ridge. Initially, a stream is below on the right and, a little farther on, there's one on your left, also. Near 0.6 mile switch back left where a path heads down to the stream on your right. Continue up past meadowed slopes to a clearing filled with lupine, pennyroyal and false hellebore, so named because of its resemblance to the European hellebore. It's a plant encountered in moist meadows and along stream banks throughout the West. It often overtakes clearings and is poisonous to livestock, which, fortunately, seldom eat it. However, early each summer as the young hellebore unfurl from their tight stalks they are robust examples of regeneration. Their vibrant green broad leaves and later their tall white tassle blooms, which justifiably gives them the alternate name corn lily, add lushness and flair to the landscape.

As you enter the clearing a noisy stream that is somewhat obscured by the dense vegetation is just off the trail on the left. At the west end of the meadow the ground cover has become solid lupine. Pass through another meadow area and then traverse up a wooded slope. Pass one last clearing just below the crest before the lake.

From the southeast end of Ridge Lake you can see the tip of Lassen Peak (No. 7). For even more views—and a particularly good perspective of the darker lava that flowed for over 1,000 feet down from the summit during the eruption of May 19, 1915—climb the steep slopes to the south and west of the lake. A more gentle exploration would be to walk along the length of the northeastern shoreline to the north end of the lake and stroll around there.

Ridge Lake

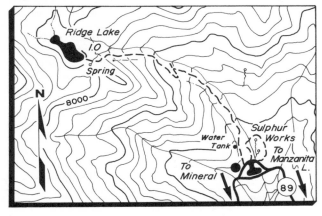

10 BROKEOFF MOUNTAIN

One day trip
Distance: 3.5 miles one way
Elevation gain: 2,600 feet
High point: 9,235 feet
Allow 2½ to 3 hours one way
Usually open mid July through October
Topographic map:
U.S.G.S. Lassen Peak, Calif.
15'   1956

Brokeoff Mountain is the highpoint on the rim of what was once a massive 11,000 foot high volcano that preceded the formation of Lassen Peak. Although the hike to the summit of Brokeoff Mountain may not have quite the cachet of the climb of Lassen Peak (No. 7), which with its 1,200 more feet is the highest point in the Park, the variety of the scenery makes it a trip that most hikers would be inclined to make repeatedly. Before the final 2.3 miles that traverse open slopes, the route alternates between deep woods and many clearings of assorted designs from lush to austere. Plus, the view from the summit is, not surprisingly, superb and includes sightings of Mt. Shasta, Lassen Peak, Chaos Crags (see No. 1), Helen Lake and across the Park to Mt. Harkness (No. 17) in the southeastern corner and Prospect Peak (No. 11) in the northeastern. Views extend south beyond the preserve over Lake Almanor to the Sierra Buttes (No. 24).

Drive on California 89 to the 2 Marker located about 0.4 mile south of the southwest entrance.

Parking spaces are off the east side of the highway and a sign on the west side identifies the trailhead.

After several yards switch back left and follow the tunnel like trail through a willow thicket. Have no trouble fording a good sized stream and soon begin meandering up through woods. Repeat the sequence of willows, ford and woods. Farther on have the first of many views ahead to Brokeoff Mountain. Pass a pond on your left and travel through a particularly good looking meadow generously filled with wildflowers. Re-enter woods void of ground cover except for limbs and twigs and then come to another meadow and cross a stream. Climb above the clearing and look down to your left for another lush, grassy area. As you enter sparser woods come to a view of Forest Lake and beyond to Lassen Peak.

People who have done the Mt. Tallac (No. 35) hike in the Lake Tahoe area from the east will be reminded of it as they make this one to Brokeoff Mountain because the trips are similar in many ways. Both begin by heading south, curving to the northwest and then climbing through a variety of terrain to a crest and following it to a rocky summit. The final distance for both is a traverse on the west side of a ridge along slopes that are much more gentle and open than those on the east side.

At 1.5 miles in a less lush, but considerably larger, meadow cross a stream, the last source of water. Traverse up in an arc to the other side of the valley and switch back twice, traveling through a zone of manzanita. Cross back to the west side of the valley and walk through stately woods. The route switch backs once, traverses at a gentler angle and then curves right and enters an area of small basins. Follow an "S" curve up through the timberline setting of scattered trees and a carpet of little lupine to the ridge crest at 2.3 miles.

Cross over to the west side and begin a 0.7 mile traverse, initially past manzanita and then along mostly open slopes. Switch back and pass some wildflowers that stand out and are especially appreciated because they bloom on an exposed, rocky slope. After traversing another 0.3 mile pass a notch in the rim where you'll have a preview of what you'll see from the top and continue the final distance to the flat summit. In addition to the panorama, you can peer down to sections of the trail you followed in.

From the summit you can visualize the size of the former Mt. Tehama, of which Brokeoff Mountain is the largest remnant, by drawing an imaginary circle that heads north over Mt. Diller and then curves southeast to Mt. Conard. Geologists aren't sure whether Mt. Tehama was worn down primarily by stream erosion, glacial action or violent eruptions.

Summit ridge of Brokeoff Mountain

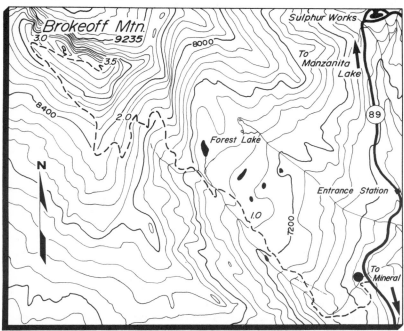

11 PROSPECT PEAK

One day trip
Distance: 3.5 miles one way
Elevation gain: 2,390 feet
High point: 8,338 feet
Allow 2½ hours one way
Usually open July through October
Topographic map:
  U.S.G.S. Prospect Peak, Calif.
  15'   1957

Although Lassen Volcanic National Park has many noteworthy characteristics, its raison d'etre is the features created by the many kinds of vulcanism. The variety of these landforms is especially obvious along the four trails (No's. 11 through 14) from Butte Lake in the northeasternmost corner of the Park. The high points in the area are two distinct types of volcanoes: Cinder Cone is an especially fine example of a tephra cone and is composed of ash, cinder and bombs. Neighboring Prospect Peak, higher but less spectacular because of its forested slopes, is also symmetrical, though with a shallower angle. However, its slopes were formed by repeated layerings of a thinner lava and is called a shield volcano. Lassen Peak (No. 7), which can be seen from all of the Butte Lake area hikes, is yet another variety—a plug dome volcano. They are formed when the lava issuing from a vent was so thick and pasty it was pushed up as one mass. Another exam-

ple of past volcanic activity is the immense jumble of black lava extending from the eastern base of Cinder Cone. A portion of this flow blocked the creek feeding Butte Lake and created Snag Lake.

The climb of Prospect Peak shares the same route as the hike to Cinder Cone for 0.4 mile before beginning the ascent. There are no water sources.

Proceed on California 44 for 11 miles southeast of its junction with California 44-89 or 43 miles northwest of Susanville to a sign identifying the unpaved spur to Butte Lake. Turn onto it and after 6.0 miles stay right, as if you were going into the campground, and leave your car across from the ranger station at the sign identifying the trailhead. Purchase one of the excellent brochures for the Cinder Cone Nature Trail. It discusses the natural history of the entire Butte Lake area and reading it will enhance any hike you make in the region.

Descend for a few hundred feet and turn right onto the Old Emigrant Trail. This route was developed in 1852 by William Noble and was a shorter, relatively easier way than Peter Lassen's, which passed east and south of the present Park boundary. As you walk over this soft surface you can appreciate the problems it caused the pioneers, already exhausted by this point.

Walk on the level for about 0.4 mile, paralleling the edge of the lava flow that forms over half of Butte Lake's shoreline, to a sign pointing left to Cold Spring at the edge of the rocks. It may be dry later in the summer and, in any case, doesn't provide potable water. One hundred feet farther along the main trail come to the junction of the spur to Prospect Peak and turn right. To be precise, the sign points to East Prospect Peak. There is a West Prospect Peak, but usually the "East" is dropped from East Prospect Peak.

Wind steadily and gradually up through woods, whose trees become even more widely spaced as you gain elevation. Also, as you climb higher the trail surface becomes firmer. Periodically, you'll have views back to Cinder Cone. Meet the edge of the shallow crater bowl at the summit and continue around the western rim to the site of the former lookout. It was removed by helicopter in 1983 and will be part of the interpretive program at Manzanita Lake. After a winter of heavy snowfall, a small lake may fill the crater floor during the first weeks of the hiking season. The mountain to the west with the lookout is West Prospect Peak, Mt. Shasta is on the northern horizon. To the south you can see major landmarks throughout the park.

The geology of any area never is simple and the crater area of Prospect Peak is no exception. Shield volcanoes usually are formed by relatively calm eruptions. However, here a cinder cone developed after the formation of the main mass of the peak.

Lookout formerly on summit of Prospect Peak (see text)

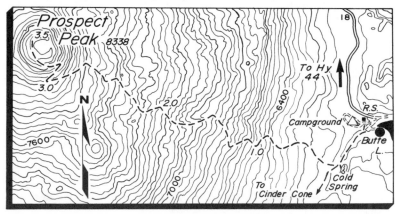

12 CINDER CONE

One day trip
Distance: 1.4 miles one way
Elevation gain: 860 feet
High point: 6,907 feet
Allow 1 to 1½ hours one way
Usually open June through October
Topographic map:
  U.S.G.S. Prospect Peak, Calif.
  15'   1957

Every area has its "A" hikes—the prime ones that shouldn't be missed—and the short climb of textbook perfect Cinder Cone is on Lassen's Best List. Cinder cones themselves are not rare but, by this time, geologically speaking, their slopes usually are forested and they don't look especially distinguished. However, Cinder Cone has no garb of trees and bushes to mask its configuration. A trail traverses up its north side and then follows the crater rim to another trail down the east and south slopes. But a close-up look at this quintessential cinder cone is only part of the hike's lure. During the climb you can see every high point from Brokeoff Mountain (No. 10) to Lassen Peak (No. 7) to Chaos Crags (see No. 1) and from the rim visible landmarks include Butte (No. 14) and Snag (No. 13) Lakes, Prospect Peak (No. 11) and lookout topped Mt. Harkness (No. 17) in the southeastern corner of the Park. Close by is the dark jumble of the Fantastic Lava Beds and the exquisitely subtle hues of the Painted Dunes. If the weather is uncommonly warm, begin in the morning, if possible. No water sources are along the hike and camping is not permitted on Cinder Cone.

One of the several options for a longer outing would be to take the trail southwest from Cinder Cone for 2.5 miles to Rainbow Lake, which is about 0.6 mile east of Lower Twin Lake (No. 4). After a possible swim at Rainbow Lake head east along another trail for 2.0 miles to the southwest end of Snag Lake (see No. 13). Walk along its west shore, where there's more good swimming, and continue north for a total of 2.6 miles to the junction of the route you took to Rainbow Lake.

Drive on California 44 for 11 miles southeast of its junction with California 44-89 or 43 miles northwest of Susanville to a sign identifying the unpaved spur to Butte Lake. Turn onto it and travel 6.0 miles, stay right, as if you were going into the campground, and leave your car across from the ranger station at the sign identifying the trailhead. Be sure to acquire one of the excellent brochures for the Cinder Cone Nature Trail.

Descend for a few hundred feet and turn right onto the Old Emigrant Trail. Walk on the level for about 0.4 mile, paralleling the lava flow that forms over half of Butte Lake's shoreline, to a sign pointing left to Cold Spring at the edge of the rocks. It may be dry later in the summer and, in any case, doesn't provide potable water. One hundred feet farther along the main trail come to the junction of the 3.0 mile spur to Prospect Peak. Stay straight (left) and continue through the open woods for 0.7 mile to a junction near the base of Cinder Cone. The trail to the right travels along the western base of the cone and is the route you'll be following back if you make the recommended loop.

Stay left and begin the traverse up the cone. STAY ON THE TRAIL. Any footprints off the tread will remain for a very, very long time, seriously marring the slope's appearance. Although the tread now is rocky rather than the volcanic ash of the first mile, the going is even more laborious. Dont't try to rush—maintain a slow to moderate pace with short, methodical steps. Soon have those promised views west to Lassen Peak and other highpoints. At the rim you can turn either direction and walk along the crest to the east side where the optional, even more scenic trail down the east and south sides begins. Before starting back, however, you could follow a short path down into the crater.

As you descend from the east rim you'll have even better views of the Painted Dunes. Travel past more rugged terrain at the southern base of the cone to the junction of the trail to Snag Lake. Turn left if you're making the loop to Rainbow Lake and then take the signed trail to the right. If not, turn right at the base of Cinder Cone. Stay right at the junction of the Nobles Emigrant Trail and soon come to the route you followed in.

Summit of Cinder Cone with Lassen Peak in background

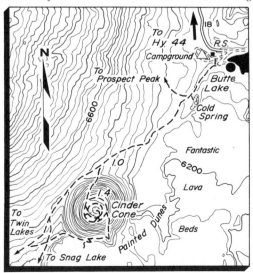

13 SNAG LAKE LOOP

One day trip or backpack
Distance: 11.7 miles round trip
Elevation gain: 900 feet round trip
High point: 6,420 feet
Allow 7 to 8 hours one way
Usually open June through October
Topographic map:
  U.S.G.S. Prospect Peak, Calif.
  15'   1957

The Snag Lake loop provides a grand tour of the exceptional formations in the northeastern corner of Lassen Volcanic National Park, most notably Cinder Cone, the immense black tangle of the Fantastic Lava Beds and Snag Lake, the second largest in the Park after Juniper Lake (No. 18). Hikers who are not planning to visit Cinder Cone (No. 12) on a separate trip are urged to make the short side loop over its summit. Backpackers should note that camping at Butte Lake is permitted only at the south end.

Proceed on California 44 for 11 miles southeast of its junction with California 44-89 or 43 miles northwest of Susanville to a sign identifying the un-

paved spur to Butte Lake. Turn onto it, after 6.0 miles stay right, as if you were going to the campground, and leave your car across from the ranger station at the sign identifying the trailhead. Be sure to acquire one of the well written brochures for the Cinder Cone Nature Trail.

Descend for a few hundred feet and turn right onto the Old Emigrant Trail. Walk on the level for 0.4 mile and 100 feet beyond a sign pointing to Cold Spring pass the start of the 3.0 mile spur up Prospect Peak (No. 11). Stay straight (left) and continue through the open woods for 0.7 mile to a junction near the base of Cinder Cone.

If you're by-passing Cinder Cone, stay right and skirt its base. Stay left at the junction of the trail to Badger Flat and pass the route down from Cinder Cone. Have a series of short, gentle downs and ups, staying left at the junction of the trail to Rainbow Lake, and then begin descending on a firmer tread to Snag Lake. A spur heads down to a beach at the edge of the lava flow, a good spot for swimming. The main trail continues in woods a bit above the lake and then farther on drops closer to water level. This section of shoreline also provides good access to potentially excellent swimming. Cross the neck of a peninsula and at an area of grassy ground cover come to the southerly trail to Rainbow and Twin Lakes.

Stay straight (left) and soon glimpse a marsh off to the left. Come to the junction of a trail to Horseshoe Lake (No. 18) and turn left. A couple tenths mile farther cross a good sized creek on a bridge and hop three smaller flows. Stay left at a trail to Juniper Lake (see No. 18), and cross another inlet stream. Pass several camp areas and then veer away from the lake through a section where lush grass thrives beneath the trees. Come near a bay on the east central side of Snag Lake and walk in a big aspen grove. Veer sharply right and have a steady, moderate mile long climb. Level off and then begin descending, losing all the elevation you just gained. From about halfway up the climb to about halfway down you'll pass the yellow-gold blooms of an astounding number of wyethia.

At 9.3 miles come to the junction of the trail past Widow Lake (No. 14). Stay left and come to a smaller aspen grove and the southern end of Butte Lake. Farther on begin traveling right against the shoreline. You'll be able to see across the lake and beyond the wall of jumbled lava to Cinder Cone and Prospect and Lassen (No. 7) Peaks. At 11 miles have an easy ford of the outlet stream. Climb in seven short switchbacks over a hump and then descend its other side. Have a few brief ups and downs and continue in the same direction to a picnic area and boat launch. Follow the road up from them to your starting point.

Along the trail south of Cinder Cone

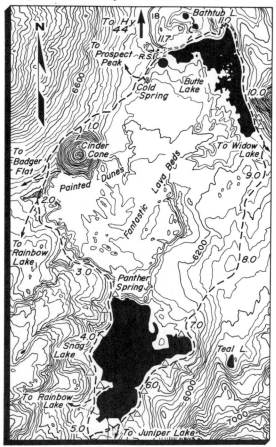

14 WIDOW LAKE

One day trip or backpack
Distance: 3.3 miles one way
Elevation gain: 950 feet; loss 150 feet
High point: 6,850 feet
Allow 2 hours one way
Usually open late June through October
Topographic map:
  U.S.G.S. Prospect Peak, Calif.
  15'   1957

The jumble of a massive lava flow called Fantastic Lava Beds forms all but the eastern side of Butte Lake. It would be the peculiar hiker who would enjoy walking far over these abrasive rocks. However, a smooth trail follows that eastern shoreline and because the southern two-thirds of the lake is relatively narrow you'll be able to look across the water to those nearby jagged chunks. Beyond that swath of black rises Cinder Cone (No. 12) and Lassen Peak (No. 7), a scene that is especially attractive later in the day when they are silhouetted.

Just beyond the south end of Butte Lake a trail veers from the main route, which continues south to Snag Lake (No.13), and climbs to the crest of the ridge and Widow Lake. As with most Lassen area hikes, you can continue farther, either from the junction to Snag Lake or south beyond Widow Lake. Backpackers could head to Jakey Lake (No. 18) and then return along either the west or east sides of Snag Lake. Note that camping is not permitted at Butte Lake, except at the south end.

Drive on California 44 for 11 miles southeast of its junction with California 44-89 or 43 miles northwest of Susanville to a sign identifying the unpaved spur to Butte Lake. Turn onto it, 6.0 miles farther stay left at the entrance to the campground and head to the parking lot for the picnic area.

Walk east from the end of the picnic area to a sign stating Snag and Widow Lakes. Continue across an open area to another sign with many mileages, have a few short climbs and descents and then a bit longer uphill to a crest. Drop from the hump in seven switchbacks and cross the outlet creek, which is no problem to ford.

The slope on your left as you follow along the lake's edge is covered with widely spaced pines and the odds are high that you'll spot some browsing deer. A few bushes and deciduous trees line the shoreline and they, combined with the large conifers, create an effect markedly different from the lava flow across the water. Already, though, some plants have established themselves on these seemingly inhospitable rocks. At the south end of Butte Lake pass through an aspen grove and a couple hundred feet beyond those attractive trees come to a junction. The trail to the right goes to Snag Lake and points beyond.

Stay left and travel at a mostly level and then moderately uphill grade through woods. Come to a clearing where some false hellebore, leopard lilies and columbines have squeezed in among the thicket of ferns. Mosquitoes can also be dense here, perhaps attracted by all those plant juices. From the upper end of this ferny meadow begin climbing more steeply as you travel beside a strip of boulders. On the way back near the top of this climb you'll have an especially attractive perspective of Cinder Cone, the Painted Dunes and Chaos Crags (see No. 1). Veer right and travel at a gentle grade for the short distance to the westernmost bay of Widow Lake. Follow the trail to a rocky area above the southwest shore. The trail continues south, passing Red Cinder Cone, and reaches Jakey Lake in about 6.0 miles.

Cinder Cone from Butte Lake

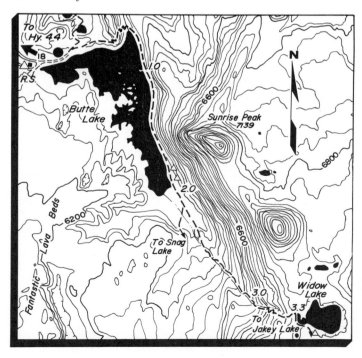

15 NORTH CARIBOU LAKES

One day trip or backpack
Distance: 5 miles one way to
Triangle Lake
Elevation gain: 600 feet; loss 100 feet
High point: 7,100 feet
Allow 3 to 3½ hours one way
Usually open mid June through October
Topographic maps:
U.S.G.S. Chester, Calif.
15'   1956
U.S.G.S. Harvey Mtn., Calif.
15'   1956

Bordering the eastern boundary of Lassen Volcanic National Park is the Caribou Wilderness. Although the latter has none of the dramatic scenery or far-ranging views of the Park, the impressive number of lakes and ponds and the complex terrain makes the Caribous a constantly pleasing area. Clumps of yellow lupine and other wildflowers line portions of the trails, pennyroyal scents the air and deer prowl among the open woods of primarily Jeffrey and lodgepole pines.

Although it would be possible to hike the majority of the trails in a day, most people would opt to make a least two visits, one through the northern half and another through the southern. Loop trips are possible in both sections. Because of the relatively gentle terrain and the frequent campsites, the area is ideal for family backpacks. Hikers need to begin with adequate drinking water and over-nighters must plan to treat all surface water. The lakes do provide good swimming, though.

If you're approaching from the south take California 36 to County Road A21, identified by a sign pointing to Highway 44, at the junction of the road down to Westwood. This intersection is 13 miles east of Chester and 23 miles west of Susanville. Follow A21 north 14 miles to the sign pointing left to Silver Lake. Coming from the north take California 44 for 29 miles south of its junction with California 44-89 or 23 miles west of Susanville to signs identifying A21 to Westwood, Caribou Wilderness and Silver Lake. Head south 4.5 miles on A21 to the junction of the route to Silver Lake.

Turn west and follow the unpaved road, along which you may encounter range cattle, for 5.0 miles. Stay right at a fork, in less than a mile turn right and then left, following signs to the Caribou Wilderness. Keep left and park. (As maps for the area show, there's also access to the northern end of the Wilderness from Cone Lake and the south from Hay Meadow but these two approaches involve more driving over unpaved roads.)

Walk along a signed trail past an outhouse to a bulletin board that gives much information about the area. Travel near the southern shore of Caribou Lake and then climb slightly to the junction of a trail to Silver Lake. Stay right, soon pass a pond populated with lilies (and mosquitoes) and continue up to a junction. If you make the recommended loop you'll be returning along the trail on your left.

Keep right and in 100 feet come to grass rimmed Cowboy Lake. Have a few minor ups and downs and then begin switch backing up the same scarp that rose above the west side of Cowboy Lake. Continue climbing, come to Jewel Lake and walk along the north shore. Travel through a little canyon, pass another pond with lilies and after a bit more uphill descend gently to a T-junction. Turn right and in a couple hundred feet come to Turnaround Lake. One mile farther pass the most easterly of the Twin Lakes and then reach large Triangle Lake, which is circled by a trail. Campsites are particularly good here.

To make the suggested loop, return to the T-junction just south of Turnaround Lake. Immediately pass Black Lake and walk along a rock walled little valley to a junction at North Divide Lake. The route that continues southwest heads into the southern section of the Caribou Wilderness (No. 16).

Turn left and after a level stretch have a gentle climb and descent to the junction on your left of the short spur to Gem Lake. Stay right and have a few tenths mile of minor ups and downs to the junction of the 1.5 mile spur up to Rim and Cyprus Lakes. Stay straight (left) and farther on make a few switchbacks down that same scarp you climbed west of Cowboy Lake. Pass near the east side of unofficially named Hourglass Lake and after several hundred yards meet the trail you followed in and turn right.

44

Campsite at Triangle Lake

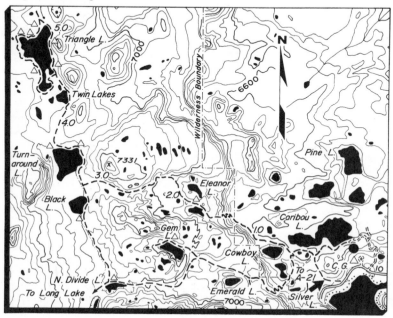

16 SOUTH CARIBOU LAKES

One day trip or backpack
Distance: 7.7 miles one way to
Beauty Lake
Elevation gain: 550 feet; loss 250 feet
High point: 7,000 feet
Allow 3½ to 4 hours one way
Usually open mid June through October
Topographic maps:
U.S.G.S. Chester, Calif.
15'   1956
U.S.G.S. Harvey Mtn., Calif.
15'   1956

The loop around Posey, Evelyn, Beauty and Hidden Lakes near the southern end of the Caribou Wilderness is probably the most scenic section of trail in the preserve. This portion has all the attributes of the northern one plus somewhat more rugged terrain. For all hikes in the Caribous begin with adequate drinking water and, if you're backpacking, include a purification system.

Coming from the south take California 36 to County Road A21 that is identified by a sign pointing north to Highway 44 and is across from the junction of the road down to Westwood. This intersection is 13 miles east of Chester and 23 miles west of Susanville. Follow A21 north 14 miles to the sign pointing left to Silver Lake. If you're approaching from the north take California 44 for 29 miles south of its junction with California 44-89 or 23 miles west of Susanville to signs identifying A21 to Westwood, Caribou Wilderness and Silver Lake. Head south 4.5 miles on A21 to the junction of the route to Silver Lake.

Turn west and follow the unpaved road, along which you may encounter range cattle, for 5.0 miles. Stay right at a fork, in less than a mile turn right and then left, following signs to the Caribou Wilderness. Keep left and park. (As maps show, there's also access to the northern end from Cone Lake and the south from Hay Meadow but they involve more driving on unpaved roads.)

Walk along a signed trail past an outhouse to a bulletin board, travel near the southern shore of Caribou Lake and then climb slightly to the junction of a connector to Silver Lake. Stay right and continue up to a junction (refer to No. 15). Turn left, pass a lake and switch back up a scarp. Stay right at the 1.5 mile spur up to Rim and Cypress Lakes and a few tenths mile farther keep left at a short trail to Gem Lake. Continue rising through complex terrain to a junction at the northwestern edge of North Divide Lake. The route to the right heads to the northern portion of the Caribous (No.15).

Stay left and, if the trail becomes faint, cross the open, marshy area at the west end of the lake. Curve left and as you approach the woods be looking for blazes on trees. Hike mostly on the level on a once again obvious tread for about 2.0 miles, passing several small lakes and ponds, to the grassy area at the north end of Long Lake and walk along its west side to a junction. If you make the highly recommended loop, you'll be returning along the trail on your left.

Keep right, following the sign to Posey, Evelyn and Beauty Lakes, hike for 0.5 mile through deep woods and cross a small clearing to Posey Lake. Continue through woods and descend slightly to Evelyn Lake. The trail goes around the southern shore and then climbs above the eastern side. Continue for 0.5 mile to Beauty Lake, descending slightly just before reaching it.

To make the return loop turn right and follow along the southwestern edge of Beauty Lake. Walk slightly downhill for 0.3 mile to a junction. The trail to your left goes directly back to Long Lake. To make the longer of the two return loops, which would add only 1.0 mile, stay right and continue slightly downhill to another junction. Turn left, walk on the level for several hundred yards before climbing to a junction just before the most southerly of the five Hidden Lakes and keep left. All have campsites but one of the best is at the most northerly lake.

Pass a pond covered with water lilies, descend and travel around the south end of a scarp. If you lose the trail along one section, keep hiking downhill and bearing left (west). Keep right where you meet the shorter loop that goes between Beauty and Hidden Lakes and in a short distance meet the trail you followed in.

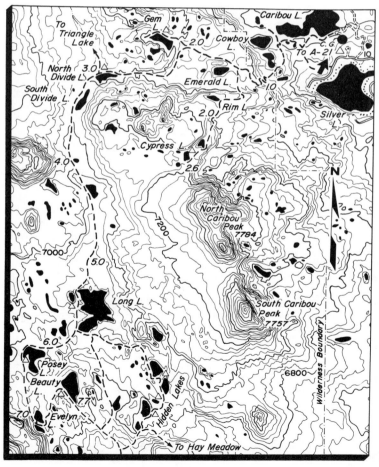

17 MT. HARKNESS

One day trip
Distance: 1.9 miles one way
Elevation gain: 1,250 feet
High point: 8,045 feet
Allow 1 to 1¼ hours one way
Usually open July through October
Topographic map:
U.S.G.S. Mt. Harkness, Calif.
15′   1956

The view from Mt. Harkness in the southeastern-most corner of Lassen Volcanic National Park provides an exceptional panorama that extends north over many landmarks in the preserve to Mt. Shasta, south to the Sierra Buttes and west to the Coast Range. The hike to the fire lookout topped summit also is noteworthy because of the dramatic change in vegetation around the 1.3 mile point from woods to vast expanses of treeless, lupine covered slopes. A loop trip, which would add only 1.5 miles, can be made by descending from the 1.7 mile point to the outlet of Juniper Lake and following its southern shoreline back to the starting point (see No. 18). There are no water sources along the hike and camping is not permitted on the summit.

At the north end of Chester turn west off California 36, following the sign to Juniper Lake 14. After 0.7 mile stay straight (right) where a road heads left to Drakesbad (No's. 19 and 20) and 5.0 miles far-

ther come to the end of the paved surface. Keep right, continuing to follow signs to Juniper Lake, and after 6.0 miles along the rough road reach the entrance to Juniper Lake Campground. Turn left and leave your car in the area marked for trailhead parking.

Walk along the main campground spur for about 175 feet to the signed trailhead on your left. The route initially climbs at a gentle grade but after a few tenths mile rises a bit more noticeably and begins an erratic series of switchbacks and meanderings. Eventually, you'll have periodic glimpses of the summit area. The crest you see actually is the east rim of the summit crater. The highest point and lookout are on the southwestern portion of the rim and you won't see them until the final several hundred yards of the hike.

After a short descent and climb traverse a slope of grass and small lupine. Re-enter woods and after a set of switchbacks come to the promised expanse of grass and lupine. From that first little clearing you traversed it appeared the route would be crossing a narrow ridge. In fact, beyond that crest are the broad, open slopes comprising the north side of Mt. Harkness. As if the scene weren't invigorating enough, you'll be further perked-up by the scent of pennyroyal. Come to the junction of the trail that descends to near the outlet of Juniper Lake.

Keep straight, continue traversing and pass the signed lightning ground wire from the lookout. Speaking of such things, on any hike get off summits and exposed ridges if a thunderstorm is building. Head for deep timber—don't huddle under a lone tree or a small grove. Have a view north beyond Brokeoff Mountain (No. 10), Lassen Peak (No. 7) and Chaos Crags (see No. 1) to Mt. Shasta. Switch back and have sightings north to Prospect Peak (No. 11) and Cinder Cone (No. 12). Switch back again and now see west across an immense canyon to the huge rectangle of Drakesbad Meadow and beyond to the white area of Devils Kitchen (No. 19). If you look a bit south from Drakesbad along the wooded slopes you may see the steam plume from Terminal Geyser (see No. 20). Make one final short switchback, curve right and walk the final distance along the crest to the lookout, which is manned during the fire season.

From the top you'll be able to see south down onto the town of Chester and Lake Almanor and beyond the Mt. Elwell area (No's. 22 and 23) to the Sierra Buttes (No. 24). If you've already done the hikes, you can identify the location of Drake Lake (No. 20) and the area covered by the route to Sifford Lakes (No. 5). Far to the west is the Yolla Bolla region of the Coast Range. You'll probably want to take some extra time to explore the crater rim.

Lookout on summit

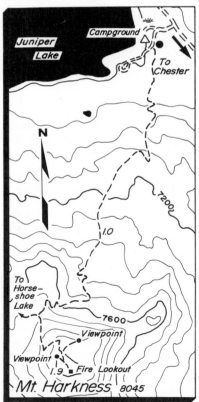

18 HORSESHOE and JAKEY LAKES LOOP

One day trip or backpack
Distance: 12.8 miles round trip
Elevation gain: 1,200 feet round trip
High point: 7,050 feet
Allow 7 to 8 hours round trip
Usually open late June through October
Topographic map:
U.S.G.S. Mt. Harkness, Calif.
15'   1956

The loop past Juniper, Indian, Horseshoe and Jakey Lakes in the southeastern corner of Lassen Volcanic National Park can be shortened into two separate circuits by following the old road between Juniper and Horseshoe Lakes. Camping at Juniper Lake is not permitted, except in the auto campground.

At the north end of Chester turn west off California 36, following the sign to Juniper Lake 14. After 0.7 mile stay straight (right) and 5.0 miles farther come to the end of the paved surface. Keep right and after 6.0 miles along the rough road reach the entrance to Juniper Lake Campground. Turn left and leave your car in the area marked for trailhead parking. (To reach the northern tip of Juniper Lake, continue along the main road another 1.4 miles to a signed area for parking.)

Walk along the campground road, passing the start of the route to Mt. Harkness (No. 17), to the far southwestern section of the loop and a sign identifying the beginning of the Lakeshore Circle. Head away from the lake for a short distance and then travel the length of the southern shoreline. Just beyond the end of the lake you can save 0.7 mile and a bit of elevation gain by heading cross-country. If you find yourself following the west shoreline, turn around and head south to the sign marking the trail to Indian and Horseshoe Lakes. People who abhor trailless travel can continue along the official tread, staying right at the route up to Mt. Harkness, turning right at the junction of the route to Warner Valley Road and then keeping left onto the trail to Indian and Horseshoe Lakes.

Climb, have a view down onto a portion of Juniper Lake and back to Mt. Harkness and after a bit more uphill begin a brief descent. Pass a lily pond on your right, resume climbing and have a glimpse of Indian Lake below. Continue up past a bigger lily pond to the signed junction of the spur down to Indian Lake.

The main trail continues up a bit farther to a crest with views of Lassen Peak (No. 7) and Chaos Crags (see No. 1). Begin descending, have a view of Horseshoe Lake and continue down to near its shore and a sign. For the next few hundred yards the tread is faint. Follow the arrow pointing to Cinder Cone via Snag Lake. Your immediate goal is the large log ranger cabin.

To continue the loop, cross a little footbridge just north of the cabin to a junction of a trail to Twin Lakes (No. 4) and turn right. Follow the charming little valley bordering aptly named Grassy Creek for 0.9 mile to a junction of a route to Snag Lake (No. 13). Turn right, have two sets of climbs and descents, cross an ample stream and a short distance farther meet the junction of another trail to Snag Lake. Turn right and soon come to the trail to Jakey Lake.

Turn left and about 0.6 mile up from the junction pass a lake and meadow. Resume climbing at an irregular, but never steep, grade. Just before Jakey Lake grass beneath the trees creates a park like setting. The trail continues past Red Cinder Cone to Widow Lake (No. 14).

To complete the loop return to the junction at 7.0 miles, turn left and soon begin climbing at an erratic grade to a broad, levelish crest. Cross it and descend along slopes of grass and exceptionally tall conifers to the trailhead. To return to the parking area near the campground, walk south on the main road, pass the beginning of the trail to Inspiration Viewpoint and just beyond it look for a sign stating Trail off the right (lakeside) of the road. Follow the tread near the northeast shore and where the trail ends at the beginning of the camp area angle left to reach your car.

Campsite at Jakey Lake

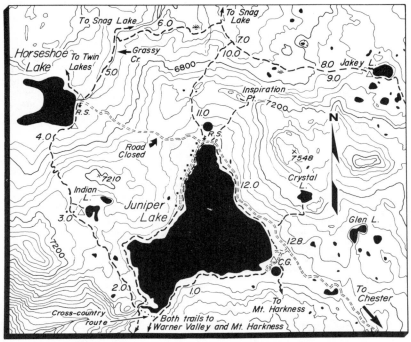

19 DEVILS KITCHEN

One day trip
Distance: 2.1 miles one way
Elevation gain: 450 feet
High point: 6,050 feet
Allow 1 to 1½ hours one way
Usually open June through October
Topographic map:
U.S.G.S. Mt. Harkness, Calif.
15'   1956

Devils Kitchen is a cozy hydrothermal area—or at least as cozy as a place like that can be—in the south central portion of Lassen Volcanic National Park. Unlike larger and considerably more frequented Bumpass Hell (No. 8) whose features are displayed in a gymnasium like setting, each steam vent and mudpot of Devils Kitchen is in its individual alcove, rather like an infernal museum. The trips to the two thermal areas are also markedly different. The trail to Bumpass Hell begins from California 89 but the one to Devils Kitchen involves driving in from the south over miles of unpaved road. Also, the hike to Bumpass Hell is along a rocky slope with a timberline setting but the first half of the one to Devils Kitchen is through immense Drakesbad Meadow with its abundance of wildlife and wildflowers.

A highly recommended loop, which would add negligible distance, can be made by returning along the trail that traverses the slope to the south above Drakesbad Meadow. Hikers wanting a longer trip could visit Drake and/or Boiling Springs Lakes (No. 20) from the loop. Camping is not permitted at Drakesbad, Devils Kitchen or Boiling Springs Lake.

At the north end of Chester turn west off California 36, following the sign to Juniper Lake and Drakesbad. After 0.7 mile stay left, as indicated by the sign pointing to Drakesbad. (The road to the right goes to the beginnings of No's. 17 and 18). Six miles farther keep right on the Warner Valley Road and in 7.0 miles come to the end of the pavement. After less than a mile pass the Park entrance, about 4.0 miles beyond it travel above a campground and 0.1 mile farther turn left onto a spur that goes to trailhead parking where there are toilet facilities. A sign listing several destinations at the southwest corner of the area identifies the trailhead. Be sure to acquire a descriptive pamphlet for Boiling Springs Lake here. It gives much interesting information on the natural history of the area.

Walk along the edge of the meadow beside Hot Springs Creek, cross the flow on a bridge and begin traversing the slope. You'll be entertained by the sights and sounds of many varieties of birds and you'll most likely see marmots and many deer. Travel above the buildings of the Drakesbad resort to a junction. If you make the recommended loop, you'll be returning along the trail to the left.

To continue directly to Devils Kitchen, stay right, descend slightly to the stream, recross it on a footbridge and then veer right to rejoin the main trail. Stay left at a fork and where the other branch rejoins a sign indicates the latter was a horse trail. A few yards farther come to the edge of the meadow and turn left. A metal sign a short distance farther indicates you're on the correct route. Walk the length of the huge meadow where you'll continue to see deer and other animals, particularly earlier and later in the day. Enter woods near the northwest corner of the meadow and rise gradually for a short distance to a junction at 1.1 miles.

Stay right and begin climbing more noticeably. Pass through an open area, climb through more woods and then cross a little meadow and stream. A few hundred feet up from the flow come to a crest and hitchrail. Descend to the beginning of the loop through Devils Kitchen. You can head either direction. Mudpot fanciers will pass one particularly fine example. As with all thermal areas, STAY ON THE OFFICIAL TRAIL.

To make the recommended loop, from the junction at 1.1 miles travel south on the level past some tall aspen, come to a good sized stream and then climb moderately to a junction. Turn right to reach Drake Lake or left to reach the trail to Boiling Springs Lake or to return to your starting point. (Refer to No. 20 for details.)

Mudpot at Devils Kitchen

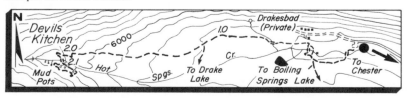

20 DRAKE and BOILING SPRINGS LAKES LOOP

One day trip
Distance: 6 miles round trip
Elevation gain: 1,065 feet round trip
High point: 6,485 feet
Allow 3½ hours round trip
Usually open June through October
Topographic map:
   U.S.G.S. Mt. Harkness, Calif.
   15′   1956

Although the hike to Drake and Boiling Springs Lakes is described here as a loop that initially travels the length of immense, verdant and wildlife filled Drakesbad Meadow, several other itineraries are possible. For a shorter loop you could skip one of the lakes or you could head directly to Boiling Springs Lake. Hikers who want a longer day outing can visit Devils Kitchen (No. 19), which would add a total of 2.0 miles, or continue south from Boiling Springs Lake for 1.5 miles to Terminal Geyser, which emits a steam plume the equal of many in Yellowstone National Park. Camping is not permitted at Drakesbad, Boiling Springs Lake or Devils Kitchen.

From the north end of Chester turn west off California 36, following the sign to Juniper Lake and Drakesbad. After 0.7 mile stay left, as indicated by the sign to Drakesbad, 6.0 miles farther keep right on the Warner Valley Road and in 7.0 miles come to the end of the pavement. After less than a mile pass the Park entrance, about 4.0 miles beyond it travel above a campground and 0.1 mile farther turn left onto a spur that goes to trailhead parking. A sign listing several destinations at the southwest corner of the area identifies the trailhead. Be sure to acquire the informative brochure for Boiling Springs Lake here.

Walk beside Hot Springs Creek, cross the flow on a bridge and begin traversing the slope to a junction. If you intend to go directly to Boiling Springs or Drake Lakes stay left here. If you plan to make the loop bear right, descend slightly to the stream, recross it on a footbridge and veer right to rejoin the main trail. Stay left at a fork and also where the other branch rejoins, in a few yards come to the edge of the meadow and turn left. A metal sign a short distance farther indicates you're on the correct route. Walk the length of the huge meadow, enter woods near the northwest corner and rise gradually for a short distance to a junction of the trail to Devils Kitchen. Turn left and walk at a levelish grade past tall aspen, cross Hot Springs Creek for the third time and climb moderately to a junction at 1.5 miles.

To reach Drake Lake turn right and continue up at a moderate grade, staying left where an abandoned trail heads right. Follow a meandering course, come to an open slope of manzanita and scattered conifers and after five steep switchbacks have a view east to lookout topped Mt. Harkness (No. 17) and, at the next turn, northwest to the top of Lassen Peak (No. 7) and down onto Drakesbad Meadow. Switch back twice more, re-enter woods and travel at a considerably more gentle grade to the edge of grass rimmed Drake Lake. Although not deep, the lake still provides a refreshing dip on a warm day.

To continue the loop head east from the junction at 1.5 miles, climb a bit and then traverse at a gentle grade. The springs shown on maps below the trail are brush covered and not obvious. Cross two streams, descend into an area of lush grass, curve sharply right and traverse the open slope to the junction with the Pacific Crest Trail at 4.4 miles.

To reach Boiling Springs Lake turn right, climb and soon enter attractive woods of big trees. Come to a junction and stay right. You'll be returning along the route to the left. Continue up at a gentle grade to Boiling Springs Lake. Follow the trail around it in a counterclockwise direction to the junction of the trail to Terminal Geyser. Turn left and walk above the north shore where you'll have views of Lassen Peak and the top of Brokeoff Mountain (No. 10). Stay right where a connector heads to the route along the southwestern side of the lake and come to the junction of the trail you followed in.

To complete the loop, follow the PCT back down to the junction at 4.4 miles, stay right and in a short distance meet the route you followed in and stay right again.

Drakesbad Meadow

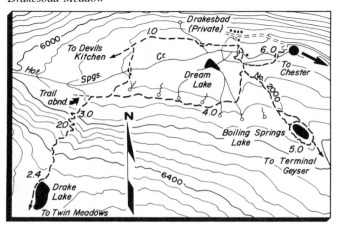

Jamison Lake

area map–gold lake

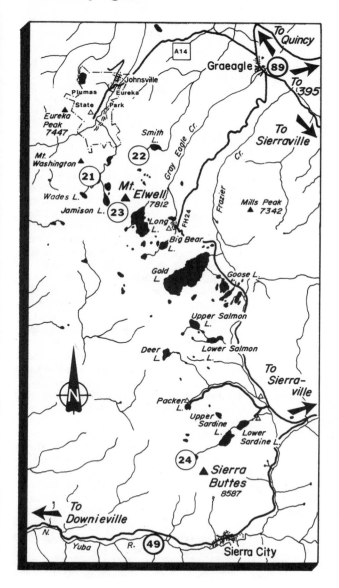

21 JAMISON and WADES LAKES

One day trip or backpack
Distance: 2.6 miles to Jamison Lake; 0.8
mile additional to Wades Lake
Elevation gain: 980 feet to Jamison
Lake; 300 feet additional
to Wades Lake
High point: 6,540 feet
Allow 1¾ hours to Jamison Lake; ¾
hour additional to Wades Lake
Usually open June through early
November
Topographic map:
U.S.G.S. Sierra City, Calif.
15'   1955

With its many lakes, pleasingly convoluted terrain and network of trails, the Lakes Basin Recreation Area (No's. 21 through 23) is an enchanting region. Note that camping is permitted only at the four lakes along this hike and at Smith Lake on trip No. 22. However, because the area is relatively small, backpackers can set up a base at one of these five lakes and explore the entire region on day hikes.

A superb little museum is near the trailhead and the hike begins at the buildings of the old Jamison Mine where much fascinating information on the area is provided. Begin with adequate water.

Proceed on California 89 to the north end of the resort community of Graeagle and turn northwest onto Road A14, following the sign to Plumas Eureka State Park. After 5.0 miles along A14 come to an unpaved road on your left identified by a sign pointing to Jamison Mine and Grass Lake Trail. (To reach that fine museum, continue on the main road

another 0.5 mile. In the past it has been open seven days a week from 8 a.m. to 4:30 p.m.) Follow the rough, but never steep, unpaved road about 1.0 mile to its end at Jamison Mine.

A trail to the campground heads right just beyond the gate. Stay left and walk past bulletin boards. Continue along an old road, passing more buildings, and curve right behind another one. Stay right where a faint path heads left and then veer left, following a sign stating Trail. After several yards stay straight (left) where a path heads down to the continuation of the old roadbed. Traverse up at a steep and then increasingly moderate angle on a rough trail to the junction of the route to Smith Lake (see No. 22), watching for marmots along this stretch. You could reach the heart of the Lakes Basin area along this route but a more scenic way is to follow the Pacific Crest Trail from above Wades Lake (see No. 23).

Stay straight (right) and soon begin walking along a considerably smoother trail. After a short, level stretch climb gradually to the 100 foot spur to a view of Jamison Falls. Pass through a grove of small aspen and continue at a gentle grade to Grass Lake. Walk right along the east shore, crossing several small side streams. At the south end pass some big aspen and then climb briefly to a meadow rimmed on its east side by fetching rock slopes. Re-enter woods, cross Jamison Creek at 2.0 miles and continue at a gently moderate uphill grade to the junction of the return loop and the more northerly trail to Wades Lake, the PCT and Mt. Washington.

To head directly to Jamison Lake, stay straight (left), climb in four short switchbacks and wend among rock outcroppings to the junction of the higher route to Wades Lake at 2.5 miles. Stay straight (left) and then come to the final fork. As soon as you turn right onto the spur to Jamison Lake you can see the rock dam at its north end a couple hundred feet ahead. Mt. Elwell is directly above to the east. To reach Rock Lake take the other branch at that final fork, cross Jamison Creek and follow a short, circuitous route among more rocks.

To make the highly recommended loop past Wades Lake, turn uphill at the junction at 2.5 miles. This route is considerably more rustic and steep than the main trail. Wind and switch back up over alpine terrain and have a view down to Grass Lake. Descend slightly into a little valley, resume climbing and enter woods, where the grade moderates. Cross the outlet stream and look for a sign on your right identifying the lake. The route you want to follow back descends from the sign. Come to the junction of the trail that heads up to the PCT and the trail past Mt. Washington. To finish the loop stay straight and continue down to the trail you followed in.

Jamison Falls

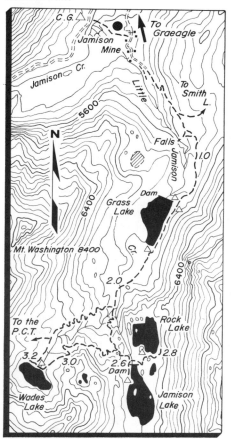

22 SMITH LAKE — MT. ELWELL LOOP

One day trip or backpack
Distance: 7 miles round trip
Elevation gain: 2,025 feet
High point: 7,812 feet
Allow 5 to 6 hours round trip
Usually open mid June through mid
    November
Topographic map:
    U.S.G.S. Sierra City, Calif.
    15'   1955

The Smith Lake—Mt. Elwell loop traverses the wooded northeastern portion of the Lakes Basin Recreation Area, crosses over the summit of Mt. Elwell and then skirts the superb lake filled heart of the preserve. On this circuit, camping is permitted at Smith Lake only. Backpackers could establish a base here and make day hikes throughout the rest of this exceptional area along the interconnecting network of trails (No's. 21 and 23). Begin with adequate water.

If you're approaching on California 89 turn southwest 1.5 miles southeast of the resort community of Graeagle onto the signed road to Gold Lake and after about 5.0 miles come to a sign pointing west to Gray Eagle Lodge.

To reach this junction from the south turn off California 49 about 5.0 miles northeast of Sierra City or 13 miles west of the junction of California 49 and 89, following the sign to Gold Lake. In 12 miles come to the road to Gray Eagle Lodge.

Turn west onto the road to the lodge, soon begin traveling on an unpaved surface and after 0.7 mile come to a junction and turn right, following the sign to Smith Lake Trail. After 100 yards stay left and soon come to a parking loop. You'll be returning along the trail marked by the sign on the southwest side of the loop.

Begin the hike from the northwest side of the parking loop at the sign that points to Smith Lake 1.0 mile. Traverse up an open slope of manzanita, eventually enter woods, cross over the nose of the ridge and descend slightly into a little inner valley. Cross Smith Creek, immediately meet a junction, turn left and soon come to a fork at 0.5 mile. To make the short side trip to Smith Lake, stay right and walk on the level to its east end. The trail travels a bit above the southern shoreline, crosses an inlet stream, passes above a large camp area and then continues west for 1.5 miles to the trail to Grass, Jamison, Rock and Wades Lakes (No. 21).

To continue the loop, take the other fork at 0.5 mile and soon begin climbing. From the signed viewpoint off the trail you can see down onto Gray Eagle Lodge and Lily Lake. At the next switchback have a view south to Sierra Buttes (No. 24). The grade moderates and the trail begins meandering up a broad slope, traveling near the edge of the breaks before curving west. Have a glimpse of Mt. Elwell and a bit farther pass near three ponds and then signed Maiden Lake, all shallow and grass rimmed.

Continue up in woods and around boulders to the summit saddle. Descend from the crest for 100 feet or so and then head left off the trail to a rocky overlook. You'll have another sighting of the Sierra Buttes and a view north to Lassen Peak (No. 7) and down onto the lakes that comprise the core of the Lakes Basin Recreation Area. As you begin descending the southwest slope of Mt. Elwell you can peer down onto Jamison Lake and look northwest across the valley to Mt. Washington.

Wind down for 0.6 mile to a junction of the route to Mud Lake and the Pacific Crest Trail (see No. 23). To continue the loop, head straight (left), following the sign to Long Lake, and continue descending. On a small bench not far below the junction where the tread may be faint make a very sharp curve left. Traverse above island dotted Long Lake on an extremely rocky tread that returns to normal near the north end. Wind among rock outcroppings and travel above a little lake. Enter woods and wind down in a grove of ferns, deciduous trees and bushes. Cross a stream and come to the junction of a trail to Lakes Basin Campground. Turn left and continue down through more deciduous woods to the spur to Fern and Hawlsey Falls. Stay left again and walk gently downhill to the junction of the route to Lily Lake and Gray Eagle Lodge. Stay left, have a wee climb and resume descending. Keep left at an unsigned fork and continue the gentle traverse to the parking area.

Maiden Lake

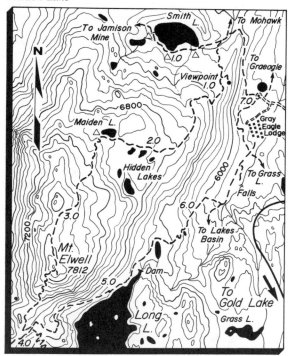

23 MT. ELWELL and LAKES BASIN

One day trip
Distance: 3.9 miles one way to Mt. Elwell
Elevation gain: 1,760 feet; loss 250 feet
       to Mt. Elwell
High point: 7,812 feet
Allow 2½ to 3 hours one way to
      Mt. Elwell
Usually open mid June through mid
      November
Topographic map:
    U.S.G.S. Sierra City, Calif.
    15'   1955

This hike through the heart of the exquisite Lakes Basin area is comprised of two loops with a side trip to Mt. Elwell. However, because of the network of interconnecting trails through this complex and condensed terrain you can create many other combinations, shorter and longer. Note that camping is not permitted at any of the lakes along this hike. However, it is allowed at all the lakes on trip No. 21 and at Smith Lake (No. 22).

If you're approaching on California 89 drive southeast 1.5 miles from the resort community of Graeagle and turn southwest onto the road marked by the sign pointing to Gold Lake. Seven miles from California 89 come to a sign identifying the road to Lakes Basin Campground and Elwell Lodge. If you're approaching from the south, turn off California 49 about 5.0 miles northeast of Sierra City or 13 miles west of the junction of 49 and 89, following the sign to Gold Lake. In 9.0 miles come to a crest at the Plumas County line and about 1.0 mile farther the Lakes Basin Campground Road.

Turn west, descend along the unpaved road, curve right and then beyond the first campsites curve left at the pay station and follow the road 0.3 mile to its end. If you plan to begin from near Gold Lake Lodge drive on the highway to the crest at the country line 1.0 mile south of the campground entrance, turn southwest onto the paved road with a stop sign and continue to a parking area.

If you're starting near Gold Lake Lodge, follow the sign pointing to Round Lake. After 100 feet come to more signs, walk along a dirt road for about 0.1 mile to a signed trail on your right and follow it to the junction at Big Bear Lake.

From the parking area just beyond the Lakes Basin Campground follow the more easterly of the two trails south for about 0.5 mile to the junction at Bear Lake of the trail from Gold Lake Lodge. Walk along the north shore of Big Bear Lake and continue up past Little Bear and Cub Lakes to a T-junction. Turn left and soon come to Silver Lake and the junction of the trail to Round Lake. Stay straight (right) and climb steadily to the junction of a trail down to Mud Lake. Turn left, following the signs to the Pacific Crest Trail. Mostly traverse up to a dirt road, turn right and follow it for a few hundred feet to signs on your right identifying the trail to Mt. Elwell and Smith Lake. If you continued straight you eventually would connect with the trail to Wades Lake (No. 21). Turn right and descend at a moderate grade along open slopes to a junction at 3.4 miles. The trail down to the right goes past Mud Lake and is the route you'll be taking if you're following the recommended itinerary.

To reach Mt. Elwell, stay straight and after a few yards turn left. The route that continues straight traverses above Long Lake (No. 22). Switch back and soon climb along a more wooded slope and near the top have a view of Jamison Lake (No.21). For the best views turn right a couple hundred feet before you reach the saddle on the summit and head to an outcropping of rocks. The trail continues north and is described in No. 22.

To complete the recommended loop wind down from the junction at 3.4 miles, following the sign to Helgramite and other lakes and then walk on the level. Where a path heads left stay right and pass near Mud Lake, a favorite spot of the range cattle that graze in the basin. Enter woods near the south end, begin winding up to the timberline setting common to the area and pass Helgramite Lake just before meeting the route you took in.

Turn left and retrace your route to the T-junction of the trail to Big Bear Lake. To complete the suggested loop, stay straight (left) and walk through a rocky little valley. Have views of immense Long Lake and then come to a short spur to it. To finish the loop, turn east (right) and wander down to the parking area southwest of Lakes Basin Campground.

Mud Lake and Mt. Elwell

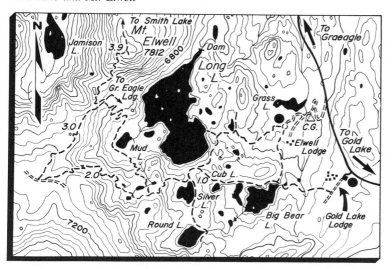

24 SIERRA BUTTES

One day trip
Distance: 3 miles one way
Elevation gain: 2,380 feet
High point: 8,587 feet
Allow 2 to 2½ hours one way
Usually open mid June through
    November
Topographic map:
  U.S.G.S. Sierra City, Calif.
  15'   1955

Although a jeep road goes to the base of the summit pinnacle from the southwest, Sierra Buttes is so impressive and distinctive that most hikers following the trail in from the north probably figure there's enough spectacle to share with those who arrive on wheels. The first half of the hike is along another rough old road that passes the Tamarack Lakes. Not surprisingly, considering the elevation gain, farther on you'll be traveling through a most pleasing alpine scene, which includes a view 600 feet directly down into the rocky basin holding Young America Lake. From the aerie of the lookout you can see Mt. Elwell (No's. 22 and 23) and, on a clear day, Lassen Peak (No. 7) and Mt. Shasta. Begin with plenty of water.

Approaching from the north, take California 89 for 1.5 miles southeast of the resort community of Graeagle to a road heading southwest and turn onto it, following the sign to Gold Lake. After 15 miles come to the signed, paved road heading right (west)

to Sardine and Packer Lakes. This junction is about 200 yards beyond (south of) Salmon Creek Campground. If you're coming from the south on California 49 drive 5.0 miles northeast of Sierra City or 13 miles west of the junction of 49 and 89 to the road heading north to Gold Lake. After 2.0 miles come to the road to Sardine and Packer Lakes.

Turn onto the road to Sardine and Packer Lakes and after 0.1 mile turn right, following the sign pointing to Trail, Packer Lake and other destinations. About 6.0 miles farther and just before Packer Lake stay left on Road 93, as indicated by the sign pointing to Sierra Buttes. In 0.1 mile come to parking on the right and a sign across the road on the left marking the route to Tamarack Lakes and Sierra Buttes.

Walk up the road and at a fork stay right, following old Pacific Crest Trail markers. Continue up along the rough bed, have a brief respite and come to a sign identifying the route left to Sardine Lakes, onto which you'll be peering later. Again stay right and pass near the more northerly of the Tamarack Lakes. Resume climbing along the road and traverse above the second lake. Begin rising at a very steep angle, intersect a road and from its other side begin traveling on a trail proper.

After 0.3 mile of traversing where one trail continues straight and another switchbacks right you can take either, because they both rejoin at the crest, but the one to the right has a better tread and more moderate grade. Come to broad crest, walk to a sign and stay left where the PCT veers off on the right. Travel along the crest and then begin meandering up in deeper woods of increasingly large trees. Artfully arranged boulders provide most of the ground cover. Come to a superb viewpoint at 2.5 miles where you can see down onto Young America and Upper and Lower Sardine Lakes and Sand Pond. (On the return you could follow the path to the left that parallels the edge. The tread becomes faint near the north end of this side loop as it curves left but just keep heading west for a couple hundred feet and you'll meet the main trail.)

A bit beyond the viewpoint travel along the edge again and then come near a road. Stay left as you walk through the area of turnouts and be watching for a white diamond shaped marker that identifies the resumption of the trail. If you miss it just continue up along the road. A trail parallels the road to the latter's north for about two-thirds of the final distance but you will have to follow the bed for the last few switchbacks to the base of the stairway up to the lookout, which is staffed through the summer until the first part of September. You can see Packer Lake, near where you began the hike, and Deer Lake above it to the north, which can be reached by a trail.

Young America Lake

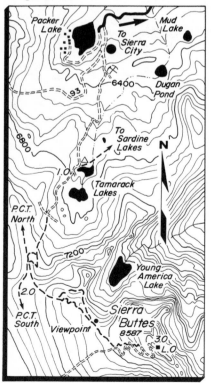

Trail to Loch Leven Lakes

area map–grouse lakes

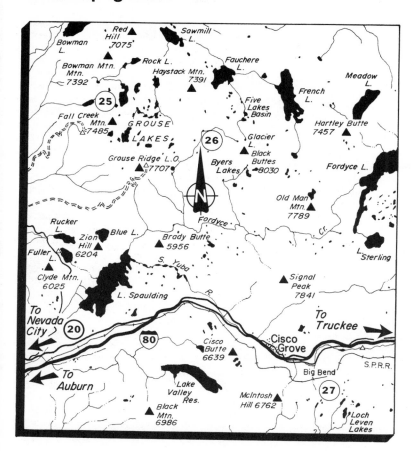

25 GROUSE LAKES LOOP

One day trip or backpack
Distance: 10.6 miles round trip
Elevation gain: 1,000 feet round trip
High point: 6,950 feet
Allow 6 to 7 hours round trip
Usually open June through October
Topographic map:
U.S.G.S. Emigrant Gap, Calif.
15'   1955

Although no Grouse Lakes exist in the Grouse Lakes area, there are more than a score with non-fowl names. Several other routes, in addition to the two (No's. 25 and 26) described here, also traverse this attractively intricate landscape but reaching them involves longer drives over rough roads.

Drive on I-80 for 16 miles west of Donner Pass or 5.0 miles east of Emigrant Gap to California 20. Take it 4.4 miles, turn right, following the sign to Bowman Lake, and then in 7.8 miles turn right onto unpaved Road 17 to Carr and Feeley Lakes.Three miles farther stay right at a fork, in 0.7 mile come to Carr Lake and continue to the parking area near the northeast shore.

Continue on foot along the road for a few hundred feet to Feeley Lake and at a fork curve left to a sign marking the start of the Round Lake Trail. (Toilet facilities are to the right.) Travel along the wooded south shore and then climb briefly. Pass a pond and a lush, grassy area and walk above an unnamed lake to the junction of the Crooked Lake Trail.

Stay right and come to a crest above Island Lake where you'll be able to see the distinctive Sierra Buttes (No. 24). After a short down and up stay left where a possibly unsigned loop past Round Lake heads right. Travel above Long Lake, stay right at the spur to it and come to the junction of the east end of that loop past Round Lake. Keep left and soon begin a sustained, but gently moderate, climb. Again stay left at the junctions of the short trails to Milk Lake and, farther on, the one up to Grouse Ridge Lookout and campground. Descend and then walk on the level to the junction of the trail to Glacier Lake.

Stay left and soon begin a long descent. Pass a little meadow and signed, usually dry Middle Lake. Continue in woods to a big meadow where cattle may be grazing and cross a wide, shallow stream and veer slightly left. If you lose the trail, walk along the west edge of the meadow for a bit and then bear left and intersect the obvious tread. Come to a sign identifying marshy Shotgun Lake. Farther on mostly descend to the junction of the trail to Sawmill Lake.

Turn left, pass a sign identifying the Bullpen Trail to Rock Lake and initially climb steeply on a rocky tread. Level off just before coming to a sign pointing the way to Penner Lake, in 50 feet come to another sign and stay left (south). After 150 feet pass a sign indicating you are on the route to Penner Lake. The connector down to Shotgun Lake, which is signed here, is obscure at its lower end. Continue south—don't veer toward Rock Lake, which you can glimpse on your right. The tread is faint for a short distance and then becomes obvious as it begins rising. Climb very steeply and near the crest turn around for a view down onto Sawmill Lake. As you descend the other side, you can see southeast into the Glacier Lake area.

Continue down to Penner Lake, cross a gulch near the northern arm and travel above, but parallel to, the lake. The route for the next 0.2 mile is not well-defined but you should have no trouble staying on course. Come to the southern arm and where a sign identifies Penner Lake, veer up to the left for 100 feet or so, travel along a little crest and begin descending on an obvious tread. You can see down over the terrain you covered north and south of Middle Lake. Pass a tarn and continue down along the slope above the Crooked Lakes, staying right where a path heads to the closest one. After some uphill drop to a marsh rimmed lake, the last of the chain. You'll have to head cross-country to visit the other Crooked Lakes—a delightful itinerary for a day hike. Travel through an area where the trees are draped with lichen to a little pass at the north end of Island Lake. Walk along the west shore and go between it and an unnamed lake to an unsigned fork. Stay left and climb for 150 linear feet to the junction of the trail you followed in.

Island Lake

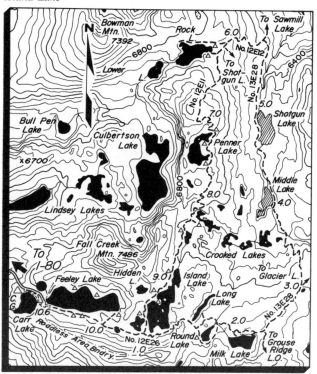

26 GLACIER LAKE

One day trip or backpack
Distance: 5.5 miles one way
Elevation gain: 900 feet
High point: 7,550 feet
Allow 3 hours one way
Usually open July through October
Topographic map:
  U.S.G.S. Emigrant Gap, Calif.
  15′   1955

For the first 3.0 miles the hike to Glacier Lake follows the same route as the Grouse Lakes loop (No. 25). The stretch from this junction to Glacier Lake and the 2.0 mile section of that big loop between Penner and Island Lake are through the most scenic portions of the region. The Glacier Lake spur passses through meadows and winds up boulder strewn slopes to the rock wall rimmed lake. Both hikers and backpackers can climb the Black Buttes above the lake or explore the more gentle terrain of the Five Lakes basin to the north. Adventuresome types could try to locate the Old Sand Ridge Trail, which allegedly follows along the crest of the ridge to the north of the lower, maintained trail, and take it back as a loop. Although it would be a long day, the hike to Glacier Lake can be combined with the Grouse Lakes loop. The entire Grouse Lakes area is crowded with backpackers on weekends.

Proceed on I-80 for l6 miles west of Donner Pass or 5.0 miles east of Emigrant Gap to California 20, which heads west to Nevada City. After 4.4 miles turn right, following the sign to Bowman Lake, and then in 7.8 miles turn right onto unpaved Road 17

to Carr and Feeley Lakes. Three miles farther stay right at a fork, in 0.7 mile come to Carr Lake and continue to the parking area near the northeast shore.

Continue on foot along the road for a few hundred feet to Feeley Lake and at a fork curve left to a sign marking the start of the Round Lake Trail. (Toilet facilities are to the right.) Travel along the wooded south shore and then climb briefly. Pass a pond and a lush, grassy area and walk above an unnamed lake to the junction of the Crooked Lake Trail.

Stay right, have a short up and down and come to a crest above Island Lake where you'll have your first view of the distinctive Sierra Buttes (No. 24). Have yet another short down and up and then stay left where a possibly unsigned loop past Round Lake heads right. Continue the irregular grade, traveling above Long Lake, stay right at the spur to it and come to the junction of the east end of that loop past Round Lake. Keep left and soon begin a sustained, but moderate, climb. Again stay left at the junctions of the short trails to Milk Lake and, in a short distance, the one up to Grouse Ridge Lookout and campground. Descend and then walk on the level to the junction of the trail to Glacier Lake. The loop described in No. 25 continues straight here and returns, eventually, along the Crooked Lake Trail.

Stay right and in a couple hundred feet come to the signed junction of the Old Sand Ridge Trail. Turn right and walk on the level through a meadow that is inexorably being taken over by trees. This is an example of a common progression. As areas of poor drainage fill with sediment, grasses and other plants thrive and eventually may completely take over. If drainage is good enough, trees will then begin encroaching on the meadow, filling the clearing just as the grasses and shrubs replaced the marsh or lake. Not all lakes meet this fate nor were all meadows formed in this manner but hikers have ample opportunities to observe various stages of this phenomenon as they tromp through the mountains. You may see, or at least hear, range cattle in the area.

Enter deeper woods and then begin climbing moderately in a forest with rocky ground cover. Enter a big meadow and pass a marsh. Farther on come to a predominantly granite area and continue up, alternating among woodsy, rocky and meadowy areas. Wind up a relatively big rock slope and at its crest veer left a bit for a view down onto the Five Lakes basin and another look at the Sierra Buttes. The trail veers to the right from the crest, descends briefly and then climbs through woods for the final few hundred yards to the lake. Water is available from a small stream at the south end of the lake.

Glacier Lake and the Black Buttes

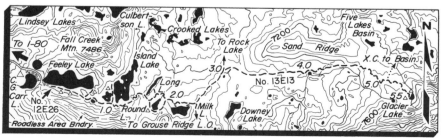

27 LOCH LEVEN and SALMON LAKES

One day trip or backpack
Distance: 3 miles to High Loch Leven Lake; 0.7 mile additional to Salmon Lake
Elevation gain: 1,300 feet; 100 feet additional gain to Salmon Lake and 100 feet loss
High point: 6,850 feet
Allow 2 hours one way; ½ hour additional to Salmon Lake
Usually open mid June through October
Topographic maps:
U.S.G.S. Cisco Grove, Calif.
7.5′   1955
U.S.G.S. Soda Springs, Calif.
7.5′   1955

Loch Leven and Salmon Lakes are among the best swimming holes in the Sierra—or any mountainous

area, tor that matter. If you have the option, make this hike in August, so you can take advantage of this uncommon feature. Although the High Sierra ambience along the final portion of the trip is at its best in sunny weather, because there are no far-ranging views, the trip is also suitable for less than perfect conditions. The trail switch backs in woods for the first 1.6 miles, crossing double railroad tracks about one-third of the way along the climb, and then travels through more open, rocky terrain as it wends from lake to lake. If you're backpacking, plan to stay at one of the Loch Leven Lakes because the area surrounding Salmon Lake is very rocky.

Drive on I-80 for 10 miles west of Donner Summit to the Rainbow Road exit, turn left, after going under the freeway curve right and head west about 1.4 miles to a sign pointing to Loch Leven Trail about 200 feet west of the Ranger Station. Park off the shoulder here—do not park on the private road. If you're coming from the west, take the Big Bend exit, 1.1 miles east of the Cisco Grove exit and continue east 0.3 mile.

Walk along the private road for 0.1 mile to a sign on the left that marks the beginning of the trail. Initially, the grade is steep but it moderates in a short distance. Briefly leave the forest and travel through a more open area of rock outcroppings. Re-enter lusher vegetation, cross a small stream on a bridge and continue up to the crossing of the railroad tracks. Wind up in about a dozen irregularly spaced switchbacks, traveling through more open woods near the end of the climb. Beyond a rocky overlook walk on the level and then gradually uphill before descending for a short distance to the first of the Loch Leven Lakes. Parallel the western shore to the junction of the spur to Salmon Lake.

To visit the other Loch Leven Lakes, turn left, after several yards climb slightly and walk along the western shore of island dotted Lower Loch Leven Lake. Because of these islands, this is the most fun lake to swim in. At the south end of the lake come to the junction of the Cherry Point Trail to Four Horse Flat. Stay left, farther on pass tiny Middle Loch Leven Lake on your left and wind up through woods and around boulders to the tip of the Upper Lake.

To visit Salmon Lake, which is considered to be the best for swimming because it's the warmest, head west from the signed junction at the first Loch Leven Lake. Climb up a slope of pines and bushes, a contrast to the deeper woods along the first part of the hike and the high alpine scene surrounding the Loch Leven Lakes. Meander down an erratic grade to the junction of the connector to Huysink Road. Keep straight (left), climb briefly and then descend in a wee canyon to the rock rimmed lake.

Salmon Lake

Watson Monument–Emigrant Pass marker

area map–donner pass

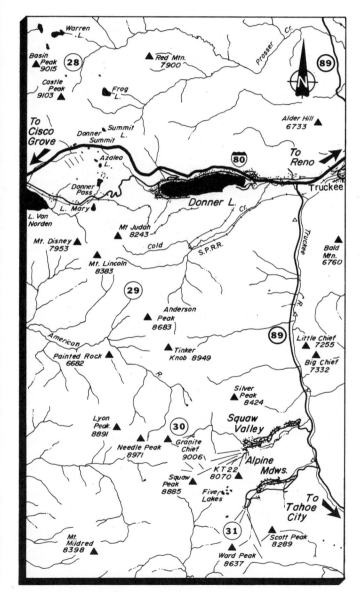

28 WARREN LAKE

One day trip or backpack
Distance: 7.5 miles one way
Elevation gain: 1,950 feet; 1,950 feet loss
High point: 8,580 feet
Allow 4½ to 5½ hours one way
Usually open July through October
Topographic map:
U.S.G.S. Donner Pass, Calif.
15′   1955

The first 3.1 miles of the hike north from Donner Summit to Warren Lake meanders up through woods and across two massive open slopes, which are filled with wyethia and other wildflowers around the middle of July, to a crest. From here you can head a few hundred yards west to a viewpoint that provides an overview of most of the hike's next 4.0 miles, a route which descends into a huge basin and then climbs to another crest before dropping to Warren Lake. Of course, although this preview only gives the gist of what you'll enjoy if you continue, it is a good stopping point for people who want a shorter hike. Additional side trips from that crest include gentle cross-country explorations west across additional open slopes toward Castle Peak and a short walk east to an overlook 1,000 feet above Frog Lake. Near the beginning of the trip there's a 0.5 mile trail to Summit Lake and from the 5.5 mile point a spur heads down to Devils Oven Lake.

Take I-80 to the Castle Peak and Boreas Ridge Areas interchange just west of Donner Summit. If you're approaching from the east, turn right at the end of the exit and follow the road up for about 250 yards to the end of the pavement and trail signs on your right. From the west, turn left at the end of the exit and go under the freeway.

Walk east (back toward the rest area) along an old roadbed to near the edge of a high stream bank, veer slightly right and parallel the stream for a short distance to an obvious crossing. From the opposite side follow a good trail to behind the rest area (where parking for hikers is not permitted). The route to Warren and Summit Lakes begins from the most easterly of the paved paths that head north from the rest area and is marked by a sign. Wind gently down through woods to the intersection with the Pacific Crest Trail and stay straight. Meander up in woods, cross a meadow packed with false hellebore and then climb a bit more to the junction of the trail to Summit Lake. It descends gently in woods, crosses open, rocky slopes that afford views south and then re-enters woods before coming to the lake.

To continue along the Warren Lake Trail stay left at the junction of the route to Summit Lake and climb to treeless slopes and a good view, particularly southeast to the Freel Peak area. Re-enter woods, hop a couple of small streams and hike up expansive open slopes to the crest. For that view down over Frog Lake and a sighting of the distinctive Sierra Buttes (No. 24) turn right at the crest and climb gradually. To see what most of the terrain between here and the destination looks like turn left at the crest. Warren Lake is behind the next ridge to the north.

Wind mostly downhill and beyond the junction of the trail to Frog Lake at a ridge crest descend into Coon Canyon directly below Castle Peak. Climb out of the canyon and traverse at an erratic grade along the tree dotted east facing slope of the basin. The route crosses several small streams and grassy patches resplendent with wildflowers. Contour along the false hellebore covered slope below Basin Peak past scattered boulders of conglomerate to the junction of the trail to Devils Oven Lake 500 feet below the ridge crest ahead. You can have a view of Devils Oven and Paradise Lakes by following the side trail until it turns sharply left and begins descending. Turn right here and walk across boulders to a viewpoint.

To continue to Warren Lake, keep right and climb gradually to the ridge top. Continue near the crest and then curve left and descend through small grassy clearings to the edge of the steep slope above Warren Lake. Wind down through woods and around rock outcroppings for 1.0 mile to a campsite at the south shore. Water is available from a creek a few yards to the west.

Pass on shoulder of Castle Peak

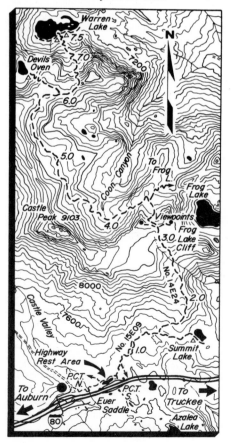

29 ANDERSON PEAK

One day trip
Distance: 5.9 miles one way
Elevation gain: 1,900 feet; loss 250 feet
High point: 8,683 feet
Allow 2½ to 3 hours one way
Usually open July through mid October
Topographic map:
  U.S.G.S. Norden, Calif.
  7.5′   1955

The trip south from Donner Pass along the Pacific Crest Trail is one of those outings where the grandiose scenery is inversely proportional to the energy needed to hike it. Or maybe the outing just seems relatively easy because visitors are so distracted by the magnificent surroundings. This section of the PCT traverses up through attractive woods for 2.5 miles and then follows along the crest of a massive, open ridge. Like the two hikes (No's. 30 and 31) farther south along the same ridge, the portion of trail from Donner Pass to Anderson Peak is over terrain unlike any other in the Lake Tahoe area.

A satisfying turnaround point is the shelter on the flank of Anderson Peak. People who get special satisfaction from reaching summits can continue on a faint trail from the shelter to the top. Hikers who opt to stop at the hut will save 0.3 mile and 360 feet of uphill. Those who prefer more gentle extensions can continue farther south along the PCT. If you have the means to establish a car shuttle, you could return along the Granite Chief Trail (No. 30) to Squaw Valley. This one way trip would be 13 miles. You also could continue along the PCT south of the Granite Chief junction and ride the aerial tram down to Squaw Valley (also refer to No. 30).

Approaching on I-80 from the west take the Soda Springs, Norden and Donner Summit Resort Area exit and follow the old highway east 4.0 miles to a big building off the south side of the road at Donner Pass. Park near the paved road that heads south just beyond the west side of the building. Coming from the east take the second Donner Lake exit west of Truckee. (By taking this second one you avoid the section along the congested north shore of Donner Lake.) Turn right where you meet the road along the lake and climb for 3.5 miles to the Pass.

Walk south down that paved road for about 100 yards to a dirt road on your left identified by a PCT sign and a hiker symbol. Turn left and follow the dirt road 100 feet to the signed beginning on your right of the trail proper. Make seven short switchbacks, with the first in vegetation and the remaining on a rocky slope. Curve around to the west facing side of the ridge and traverse over alpine like terrain of grass, rocks and trees. Switch back a couple of times and then enter deeper woods. Cross a narrow logging road at 1.0 mile and continue to traverse through woods that are open enough that they don't block the views of Mt. Disney, Lake Van Norden and other features to the west. Pass a sign marking the flank of Mt. Judah and walk at a gradual grade to a saddle and the junction of the signed Emigrant Trail to the left.

Stay right on the main route, pass a sign giving mileages to Anderson Peak and Tinker Knob and a bit farther hop a small side stream, the only easily accessible source of water on the hike. Just beyond it pass a sign identifying Mt. Lincoln and come to the beginning of that wonderful open crest. Have a short descent and climb to a view down over Donner Lake and then farther on wind down in two switchbacks. As you follow the crest you'll have views west to the Coast Range and east beyond Truckee to Mt. Rose (No. 32). Climb along slopes thick with wyethia and then have another brief descent. Walk on the east side of an outcropping of knobby rock and after yet another wee drop rise in two switchbacks. Traverse on the west side of the slope well below the crest to a saddle. The cleared swaths to the east are those of the North Star Ski Area. Follow the obvious, but unsigned, path that climbs from the saddle for 0.1 mile to the John Benson Ski Hut.

Volcanic dike near Anderson Peak

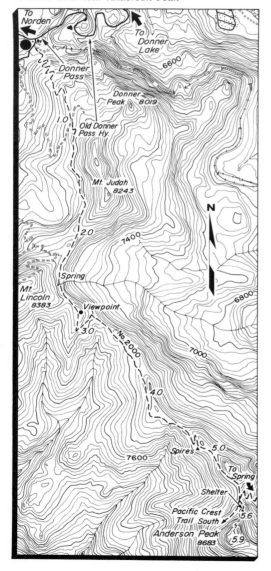

30 GRANITE CHIEF TRAIL

One day trip
Distance: 6 miles to Emigrant Pass
Marker
Elevation gain: 2,650 feet; loss 200 feet
High point: 8,700 feet
Allow 3½ to 4 hours one way
Usually open July through October
Topographic maps:
U.S.G.S. Granite Chief, Calif.
7.5′   1953
U.S.G.S. Tahoe City, Calif.
7.5′   1955

Considering all the possible variations, hardly any hiker would just follow the Granite Chief Trail up and back between Squaw Valley and the Pacific Crest Trail, scenic as this connector is. Since the PCT provides access to the upper terminal of the Squaw Valley Tram, you could make the hike one way only. A rustic route leaves the main trail at the 0.8 mile point and climbs past Shirley Lake to near the top of the tram. (If you plan to follow the Shirley Lake route, it's recommended you take it up, not down.) You could establish a car shuttle and hike south from Donner Pass (see No. 29).

Proceed on California 89 for 8.8 miles south of Truckee or 5.2 miles north of Tahoe City to the road to Squaw Valley. Turn west and after 2.3 miles curve left, cross a bridge and park in the immense lot.

Walk back across the bridge, bear left and look for the beginning of the trail at the big, brown wooden fire station sign. Traverse up the slope above the station. Try to follow what looks like the primary trail and tend to stay right at forks. Don't fret about inadvertently veering left because the lay of the land will funnel you back before the crucial

junction at 0.8 mile. Just before it you'll walk on the level through deep woods with the main stream nearby on your left. Cross a little side creek, be watching for an unsigned fork with the right branch outlined with rocks and possibly tape and turn onto it.

Wind up through woods on an unambiguous tread to a signed junction in an open area, stay left and continue climbing, eventually crossing a slope of rocks, grass and scattered trees. Re-enter deeper woods, cross over a hump and descend through an impressively dense patch of wyethia to a stream. Beyond it traverse up along the base of an imposing rock wall. The trail then rises more moderately as it travels along a wide bench of slabs. Wind up among boulders to a level area of bushes, grass and trees where the trail surface becomes smooth (and remains so for the rest of the hike). Wind up in woods for 0.7 mile to the PCT.

Turn left, continue climbing for a few hundred yards and then begin descending and have the first of many sightings of Lake Tahoe. Wind up through exquisite subalpine terrain and have a view down to Shirley Lake. Descend and walk along the edge of a meadow and then make several short switchbacks up to a saddle where a sign identifies Granite Chief. Descend for several yards to a junction where you can see ahead to the stone monument that is your destination. Stay left, continue down and then climb to the marker. The upper terminal of the tram is 1.0 mile to the east and the route down along roads to it is obvious.

If you're planning to take the Shirley Lake Trail up keep straight (left) at that unsigned junction at 0.8 mile. Stay close to the stream, where the water flows sheet like over granite slabs, climb a couple hundred linear feet farther and then cross the stream. Climb the bank to an obvious trail and turn right. Soon have a short, rocky climb followed by a level stretch and then begin rising over a setting of rocks, wee streams flowing over the boulders and pockets of grasses and wildflowers. There is no tread here but the route is reasonably obvious. Where you begin traveling at a more gentle grade and there's an old No Trespassing sign veer left and come to near the lake. Before the shore an obvious trail heads left. Take it and after it peters out turn left and climb. Curve right where you come to a bench and more or less follow the chair lift up to the crest. To reach the tram (and food) turn left and follow the road.

If you're planning to return along the PCT and Granite Chief Trail follow the road west up from the terminal, continue along a road toward the monument on the saddle just to the left (south) of Emigrant Peak, which is shown on the map as peak 8774.

Squaw Peak from Shirley Lake

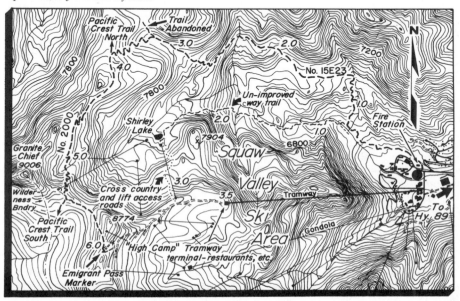

81

31 FIVE LAKES and WARD PEAK

One day trip
Distance: 2 miles to Five Lakes; 4 miles additional to Ward Peak
Elevation gain: 950 feet to Five Lakes; 1,500 feet additional gain and 400 feet loss to Ward Peak
High point: 8,637 feet
Allow 1¼ hours one way to Five Lakes; 2 hours additional to Ward Peak
Usually open July through October
Topographic maps:
  U.S.G.S. Granite Chief, Calif.
  7.5′   1953
  U.S.G.S. Tahoe City, Calif.
  7.5′   1955
Day Hiking Permit Required

The trail to Five Lakes and Ward Peak wends through the scenically varied terrain between Squaw Valley and Alpine Meadows Ski Areas and for 2.7 miles is actually in the Granite Chief Wilderness. The route turns onto the Pacific Crest Trail at the 2.9 mile point and for the final 1.5 miles traverses the open slopes characteristic of the massive ridge that extends south from Donner Pass (see No's. 29 and 30). This expanse continues enticingly beyond Ward Peak and hikers wanting a longer trip can follow south along the PCT toward Twin Peaks. You'll be joined by hordes of fellow travelers between the trailhead and Five Lakes but beyond them you'll see few other hikers.

Drive on California 89 for 4.0 miles north of Tahoe City or 10 miles south of Truckee to Alpine Meadows Road on your west. Follow it 2.1 miles to the signed trailhead on your right across from Deer Park Road, which heads down to the left.

Climb the sparsely wooded slope in traverses and switchbacks, passing through a small grove of immense conifers about midway up. The grade is moderately steep at the start but becomes more gentle farther on. At 1.1 miles come to the nose of a ridge, which looks like a pass until you actually are on it, and then climb above a rocky valley in traverses and two sets of wee switchbacks to a second quasi-crest. Pass the Wilderness boundary marker and walk on the level through woods to the junction of the 0.2 mile spur to the Five Lakes area. This trail descends gently to near the north shore of the largest lake. To visit the southwest side, continue in the same direction for a short distance until you're just beyond the northwest corner of the lake and then curve left, cross a little stream and climb slightly. No official trails to the remaining lakes, so you'll need to find your own way.

To continue to Ward Peak stay on the main trail at the junction of the spur to Five Lakes and descend, crossing a side stream, to the intersection of the PCT. Turn left and in a few hundred yards recross the creek. Traverse up a meadowed slope filled with wildflowers and make the first of 11 switchbacks. As you gain elevation, the ground cover becomes ever less and the conifers larger. Come to an open slope and switch back four more times, passing much wyethia, and then traverse along the almost treeless west side of the slope. Farther on you can see Pyramid Peak and other landmarks in the Desolation Wilderness.

Come to a saddle on the crest—a good place for a food stop because of the view over Alpine Meadows Ski Area and Lake Estelle, the terrain you covered at the beginning of the hike and beyond over Lake Tahoe to Mt. Rose (No. 32). Stanford Rock is the protuberance to the southeast. The sheer, rocky east face of the ridge you've been following, so dramatically obvious from this saddle, and the considerably more gentle and vegetated west side are characteristic of this long ridge.

Beyond the saddle come to trail signs. Leave the PCT here and climb cross-country to the first microwave installation. Ward Peak is 0.2 mile farther south along the crest. Mt. Tallac (No. 35) is only one of the many new landmarks you'll see. You'll also have an overview of the tempting terrain the PCT continues to traverse. You certainly can follow the road down from the first (more northerly) microwave installation to the ski area and walk down Alpine Meadows Road to your starting point but you probably won't save much time because the service road has many switchbacks and the terrain between them is too rough for enjoyable cross-country.

Alpine Meadows Ski Area

Summit register

area map–mt. rose

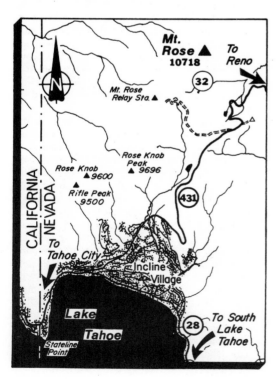

32 MT. ROSE

One day trip
Distance: 6 miles one way
Elevation gain: 2,256 feet; loss 320 feet
High point: 10,776 feet
Allow 3½ to 4 hours one way
Usually open mid July through mid
**   October**
Topographic map:
**   U.S.G.S. Mt. Rose, Nev.**
**   7.5'   1968**

What with Mt. Rose's 10,776 foot elevation and its location between Lake Tahoe and Reno, hikers know the view has to be stupendous. But based on what the massive peak looks like from a distance, hikers will assume that the price they'll pay for this panorama is a boring, long slog up barren slopes. Au contraire! The climb to the summit passes a lake, travels through a variety of woods and meadows with lush flower gardens around mid August and crosses several streams. Even the final few tenths mile, which are above timberline, are exceptionally attractive. Not surprisingly, Mt. Rose is the highest hike in this guide. Accordingly, pack additional clothing and allow extra time if you're not acclimatized.

Approaching from Lake Tahoe, proceed to the northeast shore and the junction of Nevada 28 and 431 just before Incline Village. Take 431 for 7.1 miles to a large, pinkish cinder block building and a sign stating Mt. Rose Trail on the north side of

the highway. If you're approaching from the east the trailhead is 0.3 mile west of Mt. Rose Summit.

Walk up to the west past the locked gate along the unpaved road, which is closed to all but official vehicles. Very soon have views of Lake Tahoe, huge Tahoe Meadows and the ridge of peaks, including Mt. Tallac (No. 35), forming the eastern slope of the Desolation Wilderness. Lupine, wyethia, and other wildflowers watered by several robust streams brighten the road bank on the right. Curve northwest and have a view of a microwave installation on a ridge crest, which you eventually will discover is not part of Mt. Rose. At 2.6 miles pass a grass rimmed lake below on your left and just beyond it come to a road on your right that is marked by a sign that may be on the ground. Rose Knob, which the sign indicates is to the west, is situated directly above the north end of Lake Tahoe. At this junction you'll have your first view of Mt. Rose.

Turn right, per the sign, follow the spur road and soon descend slightly into a big meadow abundantly populated with false hellebore. Before you come to a line of trees veer right onto a path that shortcuts a portion of the road. Where you meet the road again turn right and parallel the powerlines. Pass a large spring on your right that is a good spot for a snack stop and a bit farther follow the road as it drops for several hundred yards to the beginning of the trail proper on your left. Pass through that promised garden of larkspur, lupine, paintbrush and other blooms. Climb moderately and curve into a steep sided, narrow little canyon where the grade increases for a short distance—the only steepish section of the hike, by the way. Cross a stream, traverse the opposite wall, recross the flow and climb to a broad saddle and the junction of the trail down to Bronco Creek and Big Meadow.

Turn right and follow along the little ridge that connects the saddle and the main hulk of Mt. Rose. After two switchbacks on the peak itself have views northwest to Sierra Buttes (No. 24), Mt. Elwell (No's. 22 and 23) and the Grouse Lakes area (No's. 25 and 26). After three more turns you'll be able to see Donner Lake. Traverse, now above timberline, and have sightings of the peaks south of Donner Lake (No's. 29 through 31). Switch back again, traverse to the north side of the peak and have your first view of Reno. Continue traversing, make three short switchbacks and then walk along the summit ridge for several hundred feet to the register box. In addition to the landmarks noted previously, you'll be able to identify the buildings of Carson, Minden and Gardnerville, the peaks in the Sonora Pass area, Heavenly Valley, Squaw Valley and Alpine Meadows Ski Areas, Fallen Leaf Lake and, off in the distance northeast of Reno, Pyramid Lake.

Thunderstorm over Lake Tahoe from above Tahoe Meadows

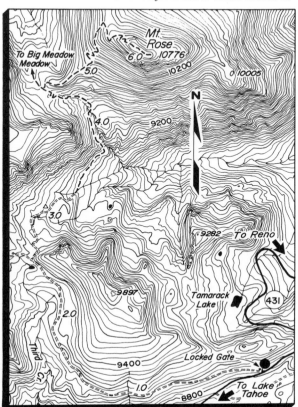

Lake Aloha

area map–desolation wilderness

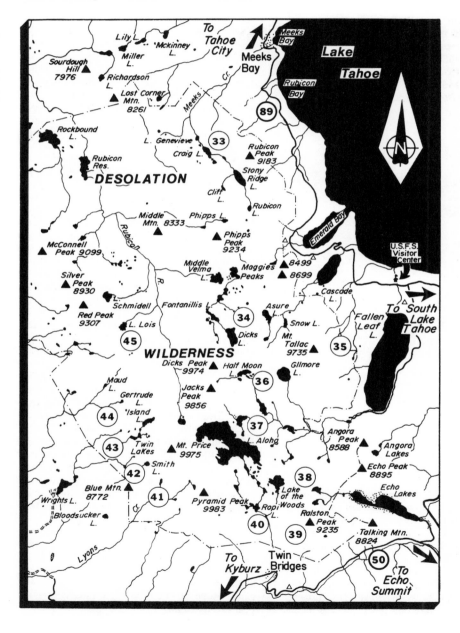

33 MEEKS CREEK TRAIL

One day trip or backpack
Distance: 7 miles to Rubicon Lake
Elevation gain: 2,100 feet
High point: 8,300 feet
Allow 3½ to 4½ hours one way to
Rubicon Lake
Usually open July through October
Topographic maps:
  U.S.G.S. Homewood, Calif.
  7.5'   1955
  U.S.G.S. Rockbound Valley, Calif.
  7.5'   1955
Day Hiking Permit Required

The Meeks Creek Trail climbs through the northeastern corner of the Desolation Wilderness past five lakes to Phipps Pass and is a good choice for a less than perfect day because the route, at least until just below Rubicon Lake, the highest one, is mostly in woods. Hikers who want to go farther over more open terrain can travel another mile from Rubicon Lake to Phipps Pass. From there the trail continues to Middle Velma Lake (No. 34) and points south. Adventuresome types can make a little return loop from Phipps Pass past Grouse Lakes back to Rubicon Lake.

Drive on California 89 along the southwest shore of Lake Tahoe to the community of Meeks Bay and look for a turnout off the east side of the highway a short distance north of the fire station and campground. A somewhat obscure sign on the west side of the highway states Desolation Wilderness and Meeks Creek Trail.

Walk west 100 feet or so to more signs and continue along the level, sandy road, which is closed to vehicles, for 1.3 miles to a post pointing to Phipps Pass and Tahoe-Yosemite Trail. Stay right and begin traversing up on a trail proper. Where a path heads down to the left stay right and continue uphill. Abruptly the forest changes from one of predominantly Douglas firs to one of pines. The trail becomes more gradual and parallels Meeks Creek. Walk on the level and travel beside a swamp of relatively recent origin, judging by the dead trees in it. Continue on the level, pass the Wilderness marker and farther on resume climbing. At the top of these windings you can turn around for a glimpse of Lake Tahoe.

Another level stretch precedes the easy ford of Meeks Creek. From the opposite side begin traversing up the slope at an erratic grade. After a levelish stretch veer sharply right, travel along a more open, rocky section and then curve left and traverse up to a post marking the junction just before Lake Genevieve of the General Creek Trail that heads west about 1.5 miles to the Pacific Crest Trail.

Stay straight (left), walk near the east shore and after a short climb come to larger Crag Lake. Beyond its south end resume climbing, cross a creek and continue up. Just past where you have your first glimpse of Hidden Lake below on your right come to an unsigned path down to it. Climb a bit more to small Shadow Lake, which supports a large lily population. Traverse up beneath tall trees along the slope of the little valley holding the outlet from Stony Ridge Lake. Walk along its west shore to a inlet stream that is a good place for a snack stop. Keep right at the fork just beyond the southern end of Stony Ridge Lake and travel above a marshy area. Switch back up the head of the valley to the western end of Rubicon Lake. Debris from the avalanche prone spring of 1986 covered a few sections of the trail along this final stretch but it may have been removed by now.

To continue to Phipps Pass continue on the main trail and, except for one slight elevation loss, climb steadily along the rocky wall for one mile to the saddle. The unmaintained loop past Grouse Lakes, visible below, heads east from the pass. You also can see a portion of Fallen Leaf Lake beyond the peaks to the southeast.

Old boardwalk across swamp

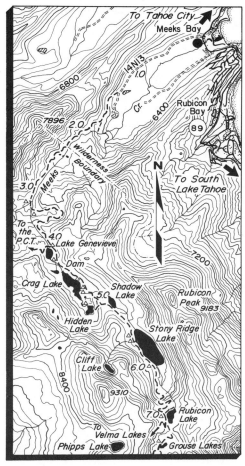

34 VELMA LAKES

One day trip or backpack
Distance: 4.6 miles to Middle Velma Lake
Elevation gain: 1,940 feet; loss 430 feet
High point: 8,200 feet
Allow 3 to 3½ hours one way
Usually open July through October
Topographic maps:
  U.S.G.S. Emerald Bay, Calif.
  7.5'   1955
  U.S.G.S. Rockbound Valley, Calif.
  7.5'   1955
Day Hiking Permit Required

The Velma Lakes are an excellent destination for both day hikers and backpackers. The latter can set up a base camp and then head north along the Pacific Crest Trail or, even more interesting, travel south over Dicks Pass to Gilmore Lake (No. 36) and points beyond (see No's. 37 and 38). Even people on a day trip may have time to loop past Fontanillis and Dicks Lake. There's also the option of returning for the final 2.7 miles along a different trail that climbs between Maggies Peaks and then descends past Granite Lake and a superb view of Emerald Bay. This way does involve 250 feet of additional uphill and a mile walk along the highway, unless a shuttle has been established. The optional loop is suggested for the return but not for taking both ways because the westerly route is more attractive.

Proceed on California 89 to above Emerald Bay and a paved road heading west that is marked by a sign stating Picnic Area, Trailhead, Eagle Falls. Follow the spur down to a large parking area. The trail begins west of the restrooms.

Climb along the rocky tread, cross a big bridge and traverse, eventually at a more gradual angle. Stay left at the junction of the spur down to Eagle Lake. The number of fellow travelers becomes considerably fewer beyond here. Have a view down over the lake and continue traversing. Enter deeper woods, cross a stream and begin winding up the timbered slope. At a fork, staying left is the preferable option. Have a couple hundred feet of faint tread and then resume traveling on an obvious trail. After a short level stretch wind up to a crest. Unfortunately, lose some elevation and then traverse to another crest and a junction. If you take the optional return route you'll be following the trail to the left.

Turn right and immediately enter terrain whose rocky, tree splashed slopes are a contrast to the woods you've just left. Mt. Tallac (No. 35) is one of the landmarks to the southeast. Meander among the outcroppings at an erratic grade to the junction of the trail to Dicks Lake. If you make the loop past Fontanillis Lake or head directly up from Upper Velma Lake you'll be returning on the route to the left.

Turn right and wander gently downhill. You'll be able to see ahead to Middle Velma Lake, which is not as distant as it seems. Pass an unnamed lake on your left, descend beside a stream and then ford it. A couple hundred feet farther come to a junction. To see Middle Velma Lake stay straight (right) and after several hundred yards of gentle uphill come to the junction of the PCT that climbs above the timberline setting of Fontanillis Lake. Stay straight and in a couple hundred feet come above Middle Velma Lake. The trail continues north to Phipps Pass (No. 33).

The trail to Upper Velma Lake winds gently uphill and then parallels the irregular shoreline. If you want to make the fun, easy semi-cross-country up from the lake, walk around to the south and then be watching for a path and blazes on your right. You'll probably be on a narrow tread for most of the climb but, as the map shows, just by heading southeast you'll intersect the Dicks Pass Trail.

To follow the optional return route between Maggies Peaks stay right on the trail to Bayview at the junction on the crest at 2.6 miles. Climb gently, more steeply and then resume a gentle traverse along a slope of widely spaced trees with no ground cover. You can see Eagle Lake, part of Lake Tahoe and Fallen Leaf Lake. Begin descending through deep woods in many switchbacks, have a view of Cascade Lake and after more windings pass above the northwest end of Granite Lake. The next switchback is at that superb view of Emerald Bay. Continue winding down to a horse loading facility and follow the road through the campground to the highway.

Eagle Lake

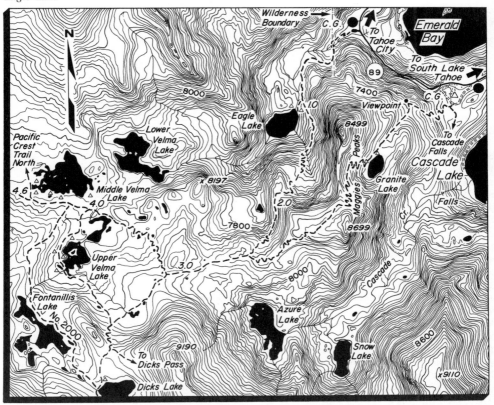

35 MT. TALLAC

One day trip
Distance: 4.6 miles one way
Elevation gain: 3,400 feet
High point: 9,735 feet
Allow 3½ to 4 hours one way
Usually open early July through October
Topographic map:
　U.S.G.S. Emerald Bay, Calif.
　7.5'　1955
Day Hiking Permit Required

Mt. Tallac, which is the Indian word for "large mountain", is the high point on the massive ridge that forms the eastern wall of Desolation Valley. For the final 1½ miles you'll have views down into this lake filled basin and from the summit you'll enjoy a panorama over much of the Desolation Wilderness plus Lake Tahoe, Fallen Leaf Lake and terrain far to the east, including Mt. Rose (No. 32). Not surprisingly, considering the 3,000 plus foot change in elevation, the trail travels in a variety of vegetation zones, from manzanita and pines through deep woods to alpine meadows and then a barren, rocky summit. Unlike the equally well situated Ralston Peak (No. 39) at the south edge of the Wilderness, Mt. Tallac is an obvious landmark. The configuration of rock gulleys on the east face of the peak is such that when filled with snow they form a massive cross that is dramatically obvious even from as far away as the northeast side of Lake Tahoe. Include a windbreaker and hat because the summit can be windy.

Drive on California 89 for 3.9 miles west of its junction with US 50 at South Lake Tahoe or about 4.0 miles south of Emerald Bay to a sign on the south side of the highway pointing north across the road to Baldwin Beach and south to Mt. Tallac, Mt. Tallac City Camp and Camp Concord. This intersection is 0.8 mile west of the road to the Forest Service Visitor Information Center. Turn south and after 75 feet resume traveling on a paved surface. In 0.4 mile turn left and 0.2 mile farther stay right, again following the sign to Tallac Trailhead, on an unpaved road that is narrow and rough but level. After another 0.2 mile come to a large parking area.

From the signs at the south end of the parking area walk along an old road for 75 yards to a post and turn right. Climb erratically beside a glacial moraine and soon have a view down onto Fallen Leaf Lake and, a bit farther, also Lake Tahoe and Heavenly Valley Ski Area. Walk along the crest of a moraine, have more views and then near 1.4 miles drop off it on the west side. Climb along a parallel moraine for a short distance before descending its west side. Rise gradually through deeper woods and come to just above Floating Island Lake. Turn left where you first see the lake to pick up the trail, which is faint for several yards. Walk the length of the lake and beyond it cross a scree slope dotted with some aspens. Continue uphill, alternating between woods and more open slopes. Cross Cathedral Creek and climb to a sign post at the junction of the old trail up from Fallen Leaf Lake. Be sure to note this fork so you don't inadvertently take the wrong branch on your return.

Continue up and come near Cathedral Lake. Immediately beyond the lake begin winding up on a considerably steeper, rockier tread. Enter a quasi-basin, cross a stream and continue up into a less lush basin where you can see ahead to the next section of trail. Curve right, traverse, switch back left where a path continues straight and climb to the crest. If you make the hike early in the season and leeward blown snow covers the final 100 feet or so you may have to leave the trail early and scramble up to the crest.

Head northwest along the gentle, grassy slope. Watch for marmots, conies, Belding ground squirrels and other rodents along this stretch. Wildflowers are in even greater variety around the second week in July.

At the junction of the trail that descends for 1.3 miles to Gilmore Lake (No. 36) turn right and continue up through slightly more austere alpine terrain for 0.2 mile and follow the sometimes obscure path over rocks for the final few hundred feet to the summit. During the periods of glaciation, Mt. Tallac, and a few of the other highest peaks in the area, were the only portions of the landscape not covered by great depths of snow and ice.

View north from Mt. Tallac summit

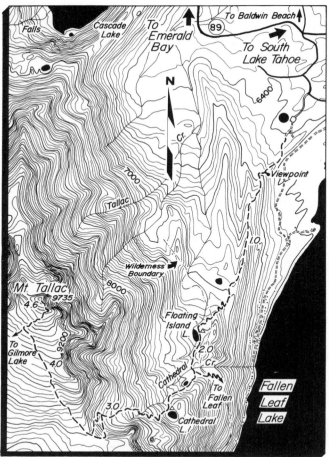

36 GILMORE and HALF MOON LAKES

One day trip or backpack
Distance: 3.8 miles one way to Gilmore Lake; 1.9 miles additional to Half Moon Lake
Elevation gain: 1,760 feet to Gilmore Lake; 230 feet additional to Half Moon Lake
High point: 8,300 feet at Gilmore Lake
Allow 2 hours one way to Gilmore Lake; 45 minutes additional to Half Moon Lake
Usually open July through October
Topographic maps:
  U.S.G.S. Emerald Bay, Calif.
  7.5′   1955
  U.S.G.S. Rockbound Valley, Calif.
  7.5′   1955
Day Hiking Permit Required

Like its downslope neighbor Susie Lake (No. 37), Gilmore Lake is an excellent place to establish a base camp from which to explore the area. You can climb Mt. Tallac (No. 35), go over Dicks Pass into the Velma Lakes basin (No. 34) or head past Susie and Heather Lakes to spectacular Lake Aloha (No. 38). There are even more possibilities if you have the time.

If you're making just a one day hike into the area it's recommended that you combine this hike to Gilmore and Half Moon Lakes with the one to Susie and Heather Lakes. The additional uphill and mileage is not excessive and the scenery around Susie and Heather Lakes, which is completely different at each one, more than makes up for the extra work.

Proceed on California 89 for 3.0 miles west of its junction with US 50 at South Lake Tahoe or

about 5.0 miles south of Emerald Bay to the road to Fallen Leaf Lake and Campground. Stay straight (left) on the narrow, but paved, road at the entrance to the campground and continue approximately 5.0 miles from the highway to the south end of Fallen Leaf Lake. Stay left, following the sign to Desolation Trails, keep left again at an unofficial sign pointing to Glen Alpine and Lily Lake and begin traveling on a rough surface. After less than a mile cross a bridge and just beyond it come to obvious places to leave your vehicle. (The route to the left here eventually meets the trail between Echo Lake and Desolation Valley (No.38).) You could drive a bit farther but the road is solid rocks.

Walk west along the road and go around a locked gate. A short distance beyond it stay on the main road where a spur heads toward the creek. Climb and then resume walking at a moderate grade to the road's end where a sign points to Susie and Gilmore Lakes. Meander up over terrain covered with rocks, trees and bushes and then in a section of deeper woods come to the junction of the 0.7 mile trail to Grass Lake.

Stay right and wind up along pine dotted rock ledges that resemble the best of the High Sierra's eastern scarp. Cross a stream at 1.8 miles, have a few more windings and then travel along the north wall of a narrow canyon. Near its head enter woods, have an easy ford of the outlet from Gilmore Lake and 150 feet farther come to the junction of the trail to Susie and Heather Lakes.

Turn right and traverse gradually uphill to the unsigned junction of a connector down to the trail to Susie Lake. Stay right and in a few feet come to another junction. The very attractive path that continues straight follows a generally level course through woods and past clusters of wildflowers for 1.0 mile. It leaves the forest, climbs along a low rock rim and then passes several ponds before coming to the eastern shore of Half Moon Lake. Dicks Pass is directly above to the north and Dicks and Jacks Peaks are the high points to the west.

To reach Gilmore Lake follow the trail up from the 4-way junction. Switch back once and as you traverse have a view down onto Susie Lake and beyond to Pyramid Peak and the expanse of rock slope above Lake Aloha. Curve left, leaving the relatively arid ambience of the slope you've just climbed, and enter a more verdant scene of grass, small trees and, around mid July, wildflowers. Climb gently to the signed junction of the route to Dicks Pass, 2.0 miles away, stay right and continue the short distance to Gilmore Lake. Unlike Half Moon, Susie, Heather and Grass Lakes, which occupy rock basins, Gilmore Lake was contained originally by a morainal dam, which has been augmented by a man made one.

Half Moon Lake and Dicks Peak

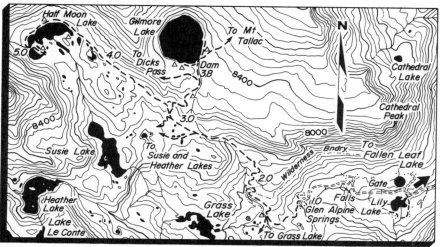

37 SUSIE and HEATHER LAKES

One day trip or backpack
Distance: 5 miles one way to Heather
      Lake
Elevation gain: 1,650 feet; loss 250 feet
High point: 7,900 feet
Allow 3 to 3½ hours one way
Usually open July through October
Topographic maps:
  U.S.G.S. Emerald Bay, Calif.
  7.5′   1955
  U.S.G.S. Rockbound Valley, Calif.
  7.5′   1955
Day Hiking Permit Required

As with several other trips in the Lake Tahoe area (specifically, No's. 34, 36, 38 and 45), Susie and Heather Lakes are excellent destinations for both a day hike and a backpack. From a base camp at Susie Lake you can make excursions past Heather Lake into magnificent Desolation Valley (No. 38) or head northeast up beyond Gilmore Lake (No. 36) to Mt. Tallac (No. 35). Nearby trails also go to Half Moon Lake (No. 36) and to Dicks Pass and beyond (see No. 34).

Drive on California 89 for 3.0 miles west of its junction with US 50 at South Lake Tahoe or about 5.0 miles south of Emerald Bay to the road to Fallen Leaf Lake and Campground. Stay straight (left) on the narrow, but paved, road at the entrance to the campground and continue approximately 5.0 miles from the highway to the south end of Fallen Leaf Lake. Stay left, following the sign to Desolation Trails, keep left again at an unofficial sign pointing to Glen Alpine and Lily Lake and begin travel-ing on a rough surface. After less than a mile cross a bridge and just beyond it come to obvious places to leave your vehicle. The route to the left here even-tually meets the trail between Echo Lake and Desolation Valley (No. 38). You could drive a bit farther but the road is solid rocks.

Walk west along the road and go around a locked gate. A short distance beyond it stay on the main road where a spur heads toward the creek. Climb and then resume walking at a moderate grade to the road's end where a sign points to Susie and Gilmore Lakes. Meander up over terrain covered with an artful blend of rocks, trees and bushes and then in a section of deeper woods come to the junc-tion of the 0.7 mile, mostly level spur to Grass Lake.

Stay right and wind up along pine dotted rock ledges that resemble a scene you'd enjoy in the High Sierra. Cross a side stream at 1.8 miles, have a few more windings and then travel along the north wall of a narrow canyon. Near its head enter woods, have an easy ford of the outlet from Gilmore Lake and 150 feet farther come to the junction of the trail to Gilmore Lake and Dicks Pass.

Stay left, continue through woods and then descend past ponds and marshes to another junc-tion. If you're intending to visit Gilmore Lake, which is no problem to include in a day hike, or any of the other possibilities to the northeast, you'll be taking the route up to the right. You could make a little loop on the return by following this con-nector up to the next junction, turning right and traversing back to the intersection just above the ford of the outlet from Gilmore Lake.

To continue to Susie and Heather Lakes, turn left, travel along the edge of a meadow and then have a short climb to the red hued rock basin holding Susie Lake. Walk along the eastern shore to the outlet creek and look downstream for a possible log crossing. On the other side veer left onto a path that heads several yards to a superb view down over Grass Lake. A faint use path descends from here to there. Retrace your steps to the main trail, turn left and follow it along the southern and southeast-ern shore of Susie Lake. You can see the dark grey rock of Mt. Tallac on the crest to the northeast. Have a brief climb over lusher terrain and then begin gradually descending through a pristine timberline setting. Cross a stream, which is an excellent spot for lunch, and a short distance far-ther come to the outlet end of Heather Lake. Aptly named Pyramid Peak, the highest point in the Wil-derness, is visible to the southeast. From the west side of Heather Lake you'll need to continue south just another 1.3 miles and climb 700 feet out of the steep sided bowl of grey rock holding Heather Lake to reach Mosquito Pass above the northeast end of Lake Aloha.

Heather Lake

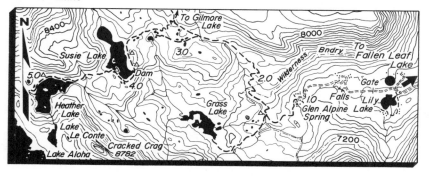

38 DESOLATION VALLEY

One day trip or backpack
Distance: 8 miles one way to Lake Le
    Conte (taking boat saves 2.7
    miles)
Elevation gain: 1,200 feet; loss 350 feet
High point: 8,360 feet
Allow 4½ to 5½ hours one way (taking
    boat saves about 1½ hours)
Usually open mid June through October
Topographic maps:
  U.S.G.S. Echo Lake, Calif.
  7.5′   1955
  U.S.G.S. Pyramid Peak, Calif.
  7.5′   1958
Day Hiking Permit Required

In all ways but geographic, Desolation Valley is the hub of the Desolation Wilderness. Trails enter it from the north, east and south and, as grand as the scenery is elsewhere, the setting of this valley, with its expanse of rock and immense Lake Aloha, is the most grandiose. By taking the boat across Echo Lake you can explore the valley on a day hike. But because of the many routes radiating from it, Desolation Valley is a perfect place for backpackers to establish a base camp.

Proceed on US 50 for 1.1 miles northwest of Echo Summit to a sign pointing to Echo Lake. Turn east, after about 0.6 mile turn left, immediately stay left and continue along the paved road 0.9 mile to a parking area on your left.

Walk down the road to the resort buildings and the dock. As of 1986 the boat operated seven days a week from 7 a.m. to 7 p.m. from around the first of June until at least Labor Day for a one way fee of $5.50 for adults, $3.50 for children.

If you've taken the boat, climb from the dock at Upper Echo Lake along the signed path to the main route. If you're hiking the initial 2.8 miles, walk across the dam north of the dock and soon begin traversing above the lake, alternating between openish and wooded slopes.

Beyond the junction at 2.8 miles climb in woods for a bit and then come to open, rocky slopes. Keep straight (left) on the main trail at the unmarked route to Triangle Lake and continue traversing to the spur down to Tamarack Lake. Stay right, farther on switch back twice and begin traveling along a meadowy slope. Stay straight (left) at the signed route to Lily Lake (see No. 37), which intersects the earlier trail to Triangle Lake, and soon begin walking on a smooth tread past Haypress Meadow to the junction of the trail to Lake of the Woods. It crosses the route between Lake Aloha and Ralston Peak (No. 39).

To continue to Lake Aloha, stay straight (right) at the junction at Haypress Meadow and travel through lush alpine terrain. Keep straight (right) at the junction of the route that intersects the trail to Lake of the Woods from Haypress Meadow and after a short descent come to the junction of the trail to Lake Lucille.

To make the little side loop past Lakes Lucille and Marjorie descend along the more rustic tread. Cross the inlet stream and 100 feet farther at a camp area look left for an unsigned path heading up. Soon parallel the inlet creek, veer away from it and come to Lake Marjorie. Turn right, look for blazes and follow them near the north shore. Climb past a few ponds in a more rocky area and meet the main trail.

Beyond the westerly junction of the Lakes Lucille and Marjorie loop, begin gently descending, have your first views of Lake Aloha and come to the junction of the trail that travels closer to its east side. Stay straight (right), traverse granite slopes, pass a pond on the left and about 200 yards beyond it where the main trail veers left (see No. 37) stay right on the unmarked path to Lake Le Conte. Where you come to Lake Le Conte turn right and follow the use path that parallels above the shore to the north end. Cross a creek and climb the 150 linear feet to the superb view down onto Heather Lake.

To reach Lake of the Woods follow the lower grade trail closer to Lake Aloha south from the 6.9 mile point. Where you come to a post stay straight (left) and about 100 feet farther come to an unsigned fork. Keep right, traverse a meadowy slope and then wind down in woods along an increasingly faint tread to the lake. Turn left and follow the path along the shore. Where you come to a big camp area, go through it and then turn left at the edge of a big meadow—don't go into it—and climb steeply along the obvious trail.

Upper and Lower Echo Lake from the trail

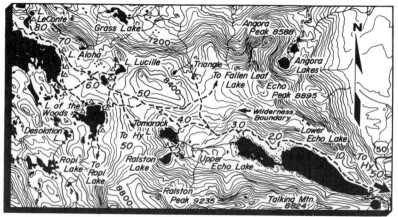

39 RALSTON PEAK

One day trip
Distance: 3.6 miles one way
Elevation gain: 2,875 feet; loss 75 feet
High point: 9,235 feet
Allow 3 hours one way
Usually open mid July through October
Topographic map:
 U.S.G.S. Echo Lake, Calif.
 7.5' 1955
Day Hiking Permit Required

In addition to being a fun hike in itself, the scene along the final few tenths mile and from the summit of Ralston Peak provides a superb view into spectacular Desolation Valley plus much of the Desolation Wilderness and the remainder of the Lake Tahoe area. This definitely is a trip to save for a clear day. The first third of the climb is in uncharacteristically deep woods, the second in more open timber with a bushy ground cover and the final along open slopes that are meadow like until the high alpine ambience of the summit ridge.

Drive on U.S. 50 for 5.7 miles west of Echo Summit or 1.4 miles east of Twin Bridges to a large area for parking off the north side of the highway across from the entrance to Camp Sacramento. A sign identifies the Ralston Trail to Desolation Valley and Lake of the Woods.

Walk northeast along a road from the parking area, stay right on the good road—don't take the steeper, rough dirt one to the left—and follow it up for 0.1 mile to a building. A sign off the left side of the road here marks the beginning of the trail proper. Wind up in woods, alternating between a moderate and somewhat steep grade. Near 0.7 mile come to an old road, walk up it—don't turn left—for several yards, curve right and resume traveling on a trail. Farther on have two short sections of downhill and traverse below a ridge crest through a thinned area. A short distance beyond where a trail comes up on the right meet a path that heads left to a viewpoint. From this overlook you can see down onto the start of the Ropi Lake (No. 40) hike, up the canyon to voluminous Horsetail Falls and beyond to Pyramid Peak, the highest point in the Wilderness.

Switch back before you come to a creek you've been hearing and wind up at a steeper grade along a rough trail. Walk on a smooth tread for a couple hundred feet beyond the Wilderness boundary marker. Have a view south to Sierra Ski Ranch and resume winding up on a steep eroded trail past those promised bushes. Just beyond the viewpoint at 1.8 miles have a brief respite in the grade and then after a couple tenths mile come to a lusher area of grass, trees and wildflowers where a path heads right to a stream. Beyond here the grade moderates and remains reasonable for the rest of the hike. Go over the nose of a ridge and then leave the timber and traverse along an open slope, losing a bit of elevation before resuming the climb. Cross two streams in meadowy areas where false hellebore are plentiful. Climb a bit more noticeably to the broad crest where you'll have views of Lake Tahoe, Lake Aloha and Lake of the Woods (No. 38), Mt. Tallac (No. 35), the other highpoints rimming Desolation Valley and, farther on, Fallen Leaf Lake.

You can continue along the trail into a hollow and then turn right onto the official route to the summit or you can turn right at the crest and follow the ridge up to where you intersect the established tread. As you gain elevation, you can see ahead to the rocky summit area and back to the Ropi Lake basin. If you walk to the north side of the crest you can peer directly down onto Echo Lake.

Adventuresome hikers might have considered combining the Ropi Lake and Ralston Peak hikes but this is not advised because crossing the dam or streams in the Ropi Lake basin is too risky in a normal year.

Summit of Ralston Peak

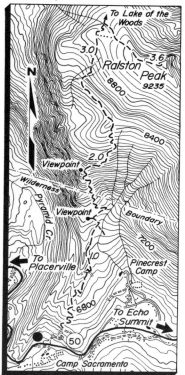

40 ROPI LAKE

One day trip or backpack
Distance: 2.8 miles one way
Elevation gain: 1,550 feet
High point: 7,630 feet
Allow 2½ to 3 hours one way
Usually open June through October
Topographic maps:
  U.S.G.S. Echo Lake, Calif.
  7.5'   1955
  U.S.G.S. Pyramid Peak, Calif.
  7.5'   1955
Day Hiking Permit Required

The hike to Ropi Lake is a classic exception to the general rule that the difficulty of a hike can be gauged by its length and elevation gain. Instead of the short, moderate workout implied by the data for this trip, the hike turns out to be one of those outings that demands as much from the brain and nervous system as it does from muscles and lungs. And it takes about as long for the descent as for the climb. The reason for all this is because 800 feet of the elevation is gained in 0.5 mile on a slope of boulders and slabs. The footing, however, is good and, except for one 12 foot pitch, there are no technical demands. Similarly, although the route is ill-defined for much of the hike, staying on course is reasonably easy. In addition to the satisfaction of meeting a modest challenge, the scenery in the basin holding the dozen or so lakes and ponds at the base of Pyramid Peak, the highest point in the Desolation Wilderness, is a generous reward for the effort.

The primary reason for doing the hike as a backpack, aside from training for some exotic expedition, would be to set up a base camp and leisurely explore the area. However, most people probably would opt for a longer day and forego hauling a heavy pack up that steep, rocky stretch. In the past, the region has attracted some messy campers, so you might include a big plastic bag and pack out some of the debris.

Proceed on US 50 for 7.1 miles west of Echo Summit or 1.6 miles east of the community of Strawberry to a turnout on the north side of the highway just west of the bridge over Pyramid Creek and east of the Twin Bridges store. A sign indicates the Desolation Wilderness is 0.5 mile ahead. The trailhead is near a private driveway so be careful not to block access to it. Since there is space for only a few cars here you may need to drive to the east end of the bridge where there is a large area for parking.

Walk across the granite slabs between two huge boulders and continue toward Pyramid Creek. Be watching for a path heading off on the left before you actually reach the stream and follow the trail. The tread is more obvious as you cross a level stretch. Although it's more comforting to be on a trail, the terrain and vegetation along this section is easy to cross-country through. Pass a metal Wilderness marker on a tree and where you come near the creek veer a bit left to pick up the tread and travel parallel to the flow. Because of the dense vegetation, you'll want to make sure you're on the trail here.

Beyond this jungle begin the promised steep climb. Essentially, parallel Pyramid Creek and try to stay within a few hundred feet of it. You'll be treated to close-up looks at impressive Horsetail Falls. As you follow the course of least resistance up the slope your distance from it will vary—just don't go too far west (left). Despite what you might suspect, the descent is no worse than the ascent and even easier if your knees are in better shape than your climbing muscles. You can turn around for views back to Ralston Peak (No. 39) and the runs of Sierra Ski Ranch. Where you come face-to-face with that big rock it's recommended that you scramble up the crack. You can go around the right (creek) side but the exposure makes this alternative far more risky.

As you near the crest the grade moderates and then is even more gradual as you approach Avalanche Lake, a surprisingly placid contrast to the forceful beauty of the falls. There continues to be no formal trail but you'll have no trouble as you head in generally the same direction past ponds and then Pitt Lake to the south end of elegantly austere Ropi Lake. Unfortunately, explorations to the east, such as the climb of Ralston Peak, usually are risky because of the voluminous outlet creeks and flow over the dam.

Horsetail Falls

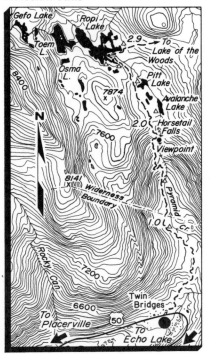

41 LAKE SYLVIA and LYONS LAKE

One day trip or backpack
Distance: 4 miles one way to Lake Sylvia; 0.5 mile additional to Lyons Lake
Elevation gain: 1,330 feet to Lake Sylvia; 420 feet additional to Lyons Lake
High point: 8,365 feet
Allow 2½ hours to Lake Sylvia; 20 minutes additional to Lyons Lake
Usually open July through October
Topographic map:
U.S.G.S. Pyramid Peak, Calif.
7.5'   1955
Day Hiking Permit Required

Five trails in this guide (No's. 41 through 45) head from the Wrights Lake area into the southwestern portion of the Desolation Wilderness. As is typical of high country hikes, proximity does not necessarily mean similarity and each of these trips has its own personality, with all of them visiting lakes as different in character as the trails to them. From south to north the hikes become harder and the terrain more rugged. Except for the trip over Rockbound Pass (No. 45), the trails end at their respective lakes, although particularly good cross-country explorations can be made from Island Lake (No. 43) and Tyler Lake (No. 44).

Most of the hike to Lake Sylvia and Lyons Lake is through attractive woods and meadows and the higher Lyons Lake is in a setting equal to any in the area. Because the route has no far-ranging views and the woodsy terrain doesn't depend on sunlight to look its best this is the recommended one of the five to make in less than perfect weather. This trip and the one to Twin and Island Lakes are especially popular with backpackers, particularly on weekends.

Drive on US 50 for 13 miles west of Echo Summit or 4.9 miles east of Kyburz to a sign stating Wrights Lake Road. Turn north and climb along the steep and winding, but paved, road. As a large sign off the shoulder explains, the obvious burn you soon travel through was started on August 8, 1981 from a vehicular accident. Four miles from the highway come to a junction and stay straight on an oiled surface. Three-tenths mile farther come to a dirt road on your right identified by a sign stating Lyons Creek Trail. Follow this rough, level road for 0.6 mile to a turnaround. The trail begins from near the southeast side of the loop.

After several feet pass some signs. The No Trespassing one is not applicable to the trail. Walk on the level or gently uphill on a mostly smooth tread through a blend of woods and meadows. Some aspen are scattered about near the beginning and the many wildflowers should be at their blooming peak around the middle of July. After 1.1 miles come to the signed junction of a trail to Wrights Lake and stay right. Continue up at a gentle, but erratic, grade, crossing several small side streams. Some meadowy patches still co-exist with the trees.

A few feet beyond an abrupt change in the character of the forest where the grassy ground cover is replaced mostly by rocks and bushes come to the sign marking the Wilderness boundary. Wind up over two bands of rocks and through woods at a moderate, irregular grade. Cross a stream, have a brief uphill stretch and then at the edge of a little meadow come to an obvious, but unsigned, fork. The trail that continues straight (right) goes to Lake Sylvia.

To reach Lyons Lake, turn left and wind steeply up the slope of rocks and trees for 0.5 mile to the pond adjacent to the outlet end of Lyons Lake. Because of its superior scenery, this is the best spot for a lunch stop. Backpackers can find the best campsites by crossing the dam and walking to the slope above the southeast side of the lake.

To visit Lake Sylvia, from the fork at the meadow walk on the level, crossing several branches of Lyons Creek. Have a brief uphill, cross the outlet from lakes 600 feet higher on the northwest shoulder of Pyramid Peak and come to the wooded west shore.

Trail sign

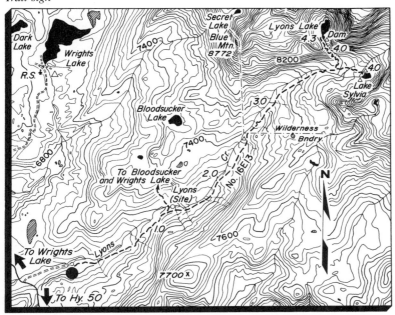

42 SMITH LAKE

One day trip
Distance: 4 miles one way (2.9 miles one
way from day hiker trailhead)
Elevation gain: 1,650 feet
High point: 8,700 feet
Allow 2½ to 3 hours one way
Usually open July through October
Topographic map:
U.S.G.S. Pyramid Peak, Calif.
7.5'   1955
Day Hiking Permit Required

Although Smith Lake and Twin and Island Lakes (No. 43) share adjacent basins—and the trails to them follow the same alignment for the first 2.5 miles—their settings are notably different. Twin and Island Lakes occupy an open, expansive setting while Hemlock and the higher Smith Lake are in small cirques. This more cozy ambience is enhanced by the lush rim of grass at Grouse Lake, the lowest of the three lakes visited on the trip, and the open woods along much of the hike. People who enjoy moderately easy cross-country travel can combine both hikes into a loop (see No. 43 for details).

Proceed on US 50 for 13 miles west of Echo

Summit or 4.9 miles east of Kyburz to a sign identifying Wrights Lake Road. Turn north and climb along the steep and winding, but paved, road. Four miles from the highway come to a junction and stay straight on an oiled surface. Three-tenths mile farther stay straight on the main road where a spur heads right to the start of the Lake Sylvia and Lyons Lake Trail (No. 41) and after 4.0 miles come to the Wilderness parking area on your right. A ranger station is to the northwest across the road. If you're making a day hike you can continue along the main road a short distance farther to a junction just beyond the bulletin and campground registration board. Turn right, stay left at the beginning of the campground loop and follow the main road past summer homes for 0.9 mile to its end where a sign points to Twin Island, Grouse and Hemlock Lakes Trail. (Refer to No. 45 for a description of the route that crosses the footbridge here.) If you're backpacking you can unload gear here but you'll have to take your car back to the Wilderness parking area.

After a few hundred feet pass through a gate and walk on the level in lush woods, paralleling a large, grass rimmed pond. Wind up in granite splashed woods and note a possibly unsigned trail coming up on your left that connects with the route to Tyler Lake and Rockbound Pass. Continue erratically up through woods of varying densities, pass the Wilderness boundary marker and travel over bouldery terrain to the junction of the trail to Twin and Island Lakes.

Turn right, walk up over granite and then wind up in woods at an uneven grade. Rise more steeply, cross a stream comprised of many little branches and continue climbing to the edge of Grouse basin. Here, and along other sections of the hike, you'll have views west to Wrights and Dark Lakes and, in the distance, Icehouse Reservoir. Walk along the shore of serene Grouse Lake and then where you leave the lake and curve left come to a fork. Stay left, pass a campsite and climb for a couple hundred linear feet to a level, boggy area. Cross the small stream here, wind up a slope of rocks, manzanita and trees and then walk through woods to Hemlock Lake around which are indeed hemlocks, identified by their drooping tips. If you're backpacking you should plan to camp at Grouse or Hemlock Lakes because the terrain at Smith Lake is rocky and sites are few.

Where you come to Hemlock Lake turn right, walk near the south shore and then begin climbing. Pass an exceptionally dense patch of heather and stay left at a faint fork that connects with that path at the northeast end of Grouse Lake. Wind up a rocky slope for the final distance to Smith Lake, which is confined on three sides by steep walls.

Unnamed peak from near Grouse Lake

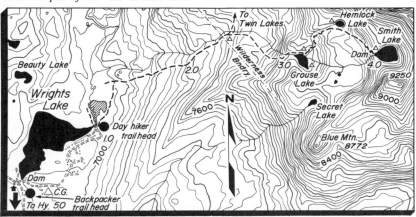

43 TWIN and ISLAND LAKES

One day trip or backpack
**Distance: 4.3 miles one way to Island
Lake (3.2 miles one way from
day hiker trailhead)**
Elevation gain: 1,215 feet
High point: 8,150 feet
Allow 2 hours one way
Usually open July through October
Topographic maps:
 U.S.G.S. Pyramid Peak, Calif.
 7.5'   1955
 U.S.G.S. Rockbound Valley. Calif.
 7.5'   1955
Day Hiking Permit Required

Of the five hikes (No's. 41 through 45) that head into the Desolation Wilderness from the Wrights Lake area the one to Twin and Island Lakes provides the grandest scenery. With its expanse of granite and pleasingly arranged vegetation this lake basin could be in the High Sierra. And considering the modest amount of effort needed to enjoy these exquisite surroundings, it's not surprising that on weekends the campsites are filled with backpackers. Hikers who enjoy moderately easy cross-country travel and have no trouble with route finding can head south and east from the 3.1 mile point to Hemlock Lake (No. 42) and then return by trail to the route they followed in.

Drive on US 50 for 13 miles west of Echo Summit or 4.9 miles east of Kyburz to a sign identifying Wrights Lake Road. Turn north and climb along the steep and winding, but paved, road. Four miles from the highway come to a junction and stay straight on an oiled surface. Three-tenths mile farther keep straight on the main road where a spur heads right to the start of the Lake Sylvia and Lyons

Lake Trail (No. 4l) and after 4.0 miles come to the Wilderness parking area on your right. A ranger station is to the northwest across the road. If you're making a day hike you can continue along the main road a short distance farther to a junction just beyond the bulletin and campground registration board. Turn right, stay left at the beginning of the campground loop and follow the main road past summer homes for 0.9 mile to its end where a sign points to Twin Island, Grouse and Hemlock Lakes Trail. (Refer to No. 45 for a description of the route that crosses the footbridge here.) If you're backpacking you can unload your gear here but you'll have to take the car back to the Wilderness parking area.

After a few hundred feet pass through a gate and walk on the level in lush woods, paralleling a large, grass rimmed pond. Wind up in granite splashed woods and note a possibly unsigned trail coming up on your left that connects with the route to Tyler Lake and Rockbound Pass. Continue erratically up through woods of varying densities, pass the Wilderness boundary marker and travel over bouldery terrain to the junction of the trail to Grouse, Hemlock and Smith Lakes.

Stay left and cross a stream. A short distance farther come to and cross a second creek. Look for the trail outlined by rocks and follow it up over the granite. Turn around for a view back over Wrights Lake. Beyond a levelish section resume meandering up over the granite, paralleling a stream whose water flows over the rock in a variety of mesmerizing cascades. Come to a crest at 3.1 miles and begin descending at a gentle grade. (This is where you'll leave the main trail if you're going to make the cross-country trip to Hemlock Lake.) Climb gently past small conifers over terrain that may be squishy until late in the summer and come to the stone dam at Lower Twin Lake. Cross it and travel above the west shore. A possible side trip would be to climb to the lakes on the top of the bench you see ahead above the east side of Upper Twin Lake. As is obvious from here,the best approach is to continue along the main trail and climb the slope that approaches the bench from the north. After you pass Boomerang Lake at 4.0 miles be watching for elephant heads, purplish wildflowers, which, close examination shows, really do have blossoms resembling that animal. A short distance farther pass an unnamed lake on your right and climb slightly to the southwestern end of Island Lake.

To make the cross-country trip to Hemlock Lake head up from the crest at 3.1 miles. From the nose of the ridge contour southeast and farther on climb a bit more—only for a few hundred linear feet—and then drop slightly to the level wooded area west of Hemlock Lake.

Hiker crossing dam at Twin Lakes

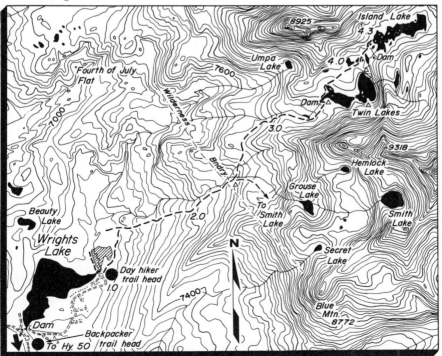

44 GERTRUDE and TYLER LAKES

One day trip or backpack
Distance: 4.7 miles one way to Gertrude Lake; 0.3 mile additional to Tyler Lake
Elevation gain: 1,265 feet to Gertrude Lake; loss 120 feet; 220 feet gain additional to Tyler Lake
High point: 8,220 feet
Allow 2¾ hours one way to Gertrude Lake; 15 minutes additional to Tyler Lake
Usually open July through October
Topographic maps:
U.S.G.S. Pyramid Peak, Calif.
7.5′   1955
U.S.G.S. Rockbound Valley, Calif.
7.5′   1955
Day Hiking Permit Required

The trail to Gertrude and Tyler Lakes is the most rustic of the routes out of the Wrights Lake area (No's. 41 through 45). Hikers who want to see more can explore the rocky, vegetated valley around Gertrude Lake and the ridges and lakes above the cirque holding Tyler Lake, visit Enchantment Pond with its South Pacific-like setting or follow an optional return loop (refer to No. 45).

Proceed on US 50 for 13 miles west of Echo Summit or 4.9 miles east of Kyburz to a sign identifying Wrights Lake Road. Turn north and climb along the steep and winding, but paved, road. Four miles from the highway come to a junction and stay straight on an oiled surface. Three-tenths mile farther keep straight on the main road (see No. 41) and after 4.0 miles come to the Wilderness parking area on your right. A ranger station is to the northwest across the road. Backpackers can drive to the trailhead only to unload gear.

Walk from the parking area to the junction just beyond the campground registration board and stay straight on the road to Dark Lake for 0.5 mile to a sign on your right identifying the trail to Maud Lake and Rockbound Pass. Hike on the level through deep woods, briefly wind up a more open slope to a crest. Have a view of Dark Lake off to your left and then descend back into deeper woods and travel along the shore of little Beauty Lake where camping is not permitted. Climb briefly to a junction, turn left, go over a rounded crest and descend to another junction. Stay straight (left), travel on the level for a bit and climb to another crest. Walk along it and have a very short descent to the junction of the trail over Rockbound Pass (No. 45).

Turn right, begin climbing on a rougher, narrower trail and farther on have a view back to Enchantment Pond and east to the pinnacles rimming the nearby basin holding Twin and Island Lakes (No. 43). Traverse gently downhill and then climb in two very rocky pitches that are separated by a short level section. Have a respite through lusher terrain and climb over a crest into woods. Meander along the slope, pass a pond and watch for where the trail curves sharply down to the left. Farther on, if avalanche debris from the spring of 1986 has not been removed, circumvent the rubble by making an occasionally soggy, but easy, arc to the right. Climb and just a few yards beyond where the route begins a slight descent come to a sign marking the 125 yard spur to the grave of William Tyler, a cowpoke who died in a blizzard here in the 1930's. About 200 linear feet up from that junction come to an unsigned fork. You can go from Gertrude Lake directly to Tyler Lake and then return from the latter along the path on the right.

To reach Gertrude Lake, stay left and after the blazes stop continue in the same direction and then veer left for a bit so you'll come close enough to the rim above Gertrude Lake that you can see it. To continue to Tyler Lake head south away from Gertrude Lake and then angle up to the southeast. You may encounter evidence of cattle, which are run in the area for two weeks late each summer.

To reach Tyler Lake by trail, climb from the junction of the spur to Gertrude Lake. Where the tread peters out bear very slightly right—you do not want to head toward the outlet creek. Where you come to the lake turn left and have an easy crossing of the outlet.

To visit Enchantment Pond leave the trail where you first saw the pool and walk down the granite slabs. Where you meet the woods at the base of the rocks turn left and head through the forest in the direction of the pond. Cross a still stream twice and come to the pool. Return to where the granite and woods meet and head northwest until you intersect the main trail.

William Tyler's grave

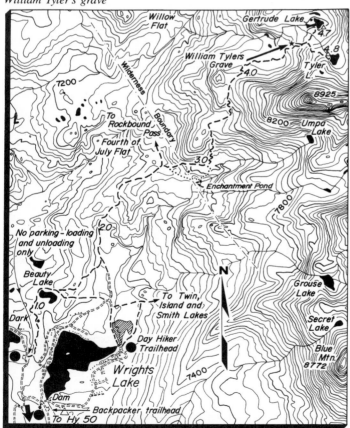

45 ROCKBOUND PASS

One day trip or backpack
Distance: 5.7 miles one way to Rock-
bound Pass; 2.8 miles addi-
tional to Lake Schmidell
Elevation gain: 1,670 feet; loss 120 feet;
160 feet additional gain
and 850 feet loss to Lake
Schmidell
High point: 8,550 feet
Allow 3 hours one way; 1¼ hours addi-
tional to Lake Schmidell
Usually open July through October
Topographic maps:
U.S.G.S. Pyramid Peak, Calif.
7.5′   1955
U.S.G.S. Rockbound Pass, Calif.
7.5′   1955
Day Hiking Permit Required

The climb to Rockbound Pass is the most northerly of the four hikes (No's. 42 through 45) that begin at Wrights Lake. People who want a longer day trip and backpackers can continue down from the crest for an additional 2.8 miles through one of the best wildflower displays in the Desolation Wilderness past Lakes Doris and Lois to large Lake Schmidell. The latter is an excellent place to establish a base camp from which to follow lesser traveled routes into the northern half of the preserve. The hikes to Rockbound Pass and Gertrude and Tyler Lakes follow the same alignment for the first 2.6 miles.

Drive on US 50 for 13 miles west of Echo Summit or 4.9 miles east of Kyburz to a sign identifying Wrights Lake Road. Turn north and climb along the steep and winding, but paved, road. Four miles from the highway come to a junction and stay straight on an oiled surface. Three-tenths mile farther keep straight on the main road where a spur heads right (see No. 41) and after 4.0 miles come to the Wilderness parking area on your right. A ranger station is to the northwest across the road. Backpackers and hikers can drive to the trailhead only to unload gear.

Walk from the parking area to the junction just beyond the bulletin and campground registration board and stay straight on the road to Dark Lake for 0.5 mile to a sign on your right identifying the trail to Maud Lake and Rockbound Pass. Hike on the level through deep woods, briefly wind up a more open slope to a crest and climb gently along it. Have a view of Dark Lake off to your left and then descend back into deeper woods and travel along the shore of little Beauty Lake where camping is not permitted. Climb briefly to a junction, turn left and continue up to a rounded crest and then descend to another junction at 1.7 miles. You could return along the route to the right here.

Stay straight (left), travel on the level for a bit and then climb to another little ridge top. Walk along it and have a very short descent to the junction of the route to Gertrude and Tyler Lakes. Stay left again and travel through woods before resuming hiking in more open terrain. Climb slightly and then descend to the crossing of Silver Creek. As the trail curves to the northeast you can see ahead to Rockbound Pass, the notch on the crest that is bordered on the south by reddish colored rock. Hike up granite slabs and then pass through a willow thicket and a small forest before coming to the junction of the trail to Lawrence Lake. Keep right and switch back up the trail that has been blasted out of rock to the level area around irregularly shaped Maud Lake.

The trail continues around the northwest side of the lake and rises sporadically through small grassy areas for about 0.4 mile before beginning the 0.6 mile steady climb to wide Rockbound Pass. From it you can see back to Maud Lake and north down to Lake Doris.

The trail past Lakes Doris and Lois meanders gently downhill or on the level and travels through many lush areas. However, you'll have a short climb and then a 560 foot drop for the final 1.5 miles to Lake Schmidell.

To make that optional return loop along the east end of Wrights Lake, stay straight (left) at the junction at 1.7 miles, following the sign to Summer Homes. Walk along an old roadbed, at a cattle guard veer very slightly left, continuing on the road, and soon pass a sign on your left marking the trail up to Twin and Island Lakes (No. 43). Cross a high footbridge over the grass rimmed, canal like inlet and come to a small parking area for day hikers (No. 42). Walk along the road past summer homes, stay right at the campground entrance and continue to the junction with the road you took in.

114

Maud Lake

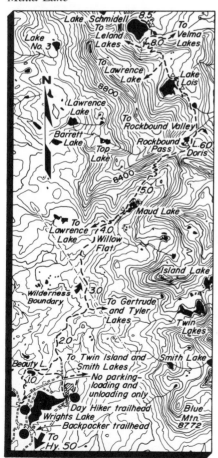

ON THIS SPOT, WHICH MARKS THE SUMMIT OF THE KIT CARSON PASS, STOOD WHAT WAS KNOWN AS THE KIT CARSON TREE ON WHICH THE FAMOUS SCOUT KIT CARSON INSCRIBED HIS NAME IN 1844 WHEN HE GUIDED THE THEN CAPTAIN JOHN C. FREMONT, HEAD OF A GOVERNMENT EXPLORING EXPEDITION, OVER THE SIERRA NEVADA MOUNTAINS. ABOVE IS A REPLICA OF THE ORIGINAL INSCRIPTION CUT FROM THE TREE IN 1888 AND NOW IN SUTTER'S FORT, SACRAMENTO.

ERECTED BY HISTORIC LANDMARKS COMMITTEE, NATIVE SONS OF THE GOLDEN WEST, 1921.

area map–carson pass

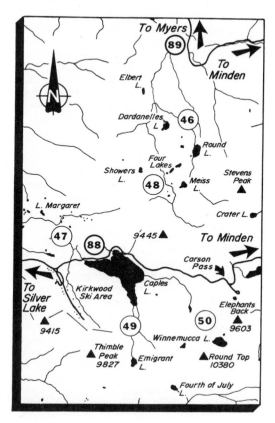

46 DARDANELLES and ROUND LAKES

One day trip or backpack
Distance: 4 miles one way to Dardanelles Lake; 0.7 mile additional to Round Lake
Elevation gain: 990 feet; loss 430 feet to Dardanelles Lake; 290 feet additional gain to Round Lake
High point: 8,080 feet
Allow 2 to 2½ hours one way to Dardanelles Lake; 20 minutes additional to Round Lake
Usually open July through October
Topographic maps:
    U.S.G.S. Echo Lake, Calif.
    7.5'   1955
    U.S.G.S. Freel Peak, Calif.
    7.5'   1955

Although every hike has its own personality, throughout a geographic area there's usually a family resemblance among the various trails. But there are always a few routes that just don't look much like their brethren and the hike to Dardanelles and Round Lakes—and Round Lake itself—is one of these exceptions. Near the beginning you'll cross an immense meadow—not just a valley floor or an open slope—that has, in the past, supported an equally large herd of placid cattle. Some sagebrush dot the shore of Round Lake and a cliff of knobby rocks rises above the east side. Dardanelles Lake, however, does have the more conventional setting of trees, boulders and granite slabs.

If you're backpacking and intend to make day excursions, the most efficient location for a base camp is Round Lake, although it is slightly less attractive than Dardanelles Lake. From it you can continue south to a long, broad valley and follow a scenic section of the Pacific Crest Trail south to Meiss Pass or north to Showers Lake (No. 48), where you'll have a view 900 feet down to Dardanelles Lake.

Because there are no far-ranging views, this hike is a good choice for a gloomy day. But if you're here on a warm day later in the summer plan on a swim in Round Lake, which is uncharacteristically temperate. Begin with adequate drinking water and include a purification system if you're backpacking.

Proceed on California 89 for 5.0 miles south of its junction with US 50 at Meyers or 6.1 miles north of its intersection with California 88 to a pullout off the north shoulder. The trail begins across the highway and the signs that mark it are somewhat obscured by trees as you approach from the north.

Wind up in woods for about 0.4 mile to a maze like barrier and 100 yards beyond it come to Big Meadow. For a log crossing of the stream take the path that forks to the right and then head south across the meadow. Both stakes and a tread identify the route. Of course, don't harass the cattle and prevent any dogs you might have with you from doing so, too. Re-enter woods at the south end of the meadow and resume climbing. Eventually, traverse up more open slopes of lupine, wyethia, pennyroyal and small bushes and then cross a larger, more verdant swath filled with false hellebore. Once again travel in deeper woods and just before you come to the crest cross a log cattle guard. Traverse down the other side of the ridge to a junction where a sign points ahead to Round Lake and right to Christmas Valley. Some always lovely aspen thrive near this intersection.

To reach Dardanelles Lake, turn right and descend gradually for 0.2 mile to an unsigned , but obvious, junction on your left. Turn left, have an easy ford of the stream and soon cross a second creek. Pass a pond that supports many lily pads and then descend at a gentle to moderate grade through lush, pretty woods, whose floor is sprinkled with larkspur and other wildflowers. Cross a third stream, a fork of the Upper Truckee River, and wind up among small rock outcroppings—an abrupt change in scenery. Level off and re-enter woods. The main trail dead ends near a camp area. You can head west from here for a couple hundred feet to the lake or retrace your route a bit and follow one of the side paths that leave the main route.

To visit Round Lake, and points beyond, continue south from the junction at 2.4 miles. The trail climbs slightly and then descends and winds through an area of large boulders of conglomerate before coming to the northeast shore of the lake.

Big Meadow

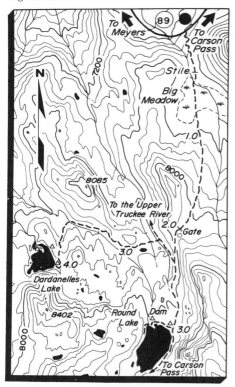

est wall. At the end of both these
im "Wow!", or something similar.
but entirely charming, the tread to
follows close to the shore of Caples
n climbs through deep woods and
ows. This trip generates a feeling of

n you return from the trip to Lake
you'll probably mentally chuckle. Be
his hike is just fine: it travels through a
dow and a grove of huge aspen, visits two
d a pond and goes over some proper Sierra
And it's a perfect length for when you don't
he time or inclination for a strenuous hike.
se there are no far-ranging views or exposed
ons, it's also good for less than perfect weather.
it nevertheless bemuses. At the beginning, you
skeptical that a lake could even exist on those
pes ahead. The tread is well defined at the begin-
ing and then farther on where it goes over granite
labs it is not marked at all. The creek at 0.5 mile
is spanned by a very wide bridge but the one at 1.9
miles has only a broken log. But that second stream
and the rocky portions present no problems—they
just contribute to this hike's slightly peculiar
personality.

Drive on California 88 for 5.2 miles west of
Carson Pass or about 5.5 miles east of Silver Lake
to a sign 0.2 mile below the spillway at Caples Lake
pointing to Lake Margaret. Turn north and follow
the road 200 feet to a trail sign on your left and
a few parking spaces.

Wind down a rocky slope scattered with conifers
into deeper woods. Level off, cross a small stream
and soon pass an oxbow of Caples Creek on your
left. Walk along the edge of a big meadow and cross
the flow on that wide bridge. After a bit more level
begin climbing at a gentle to moderate angle over
terrain of trees and scattered boulders. The
remainder of the hike you'll be alternating among
sections of level, uphill and downhill.

Pass a pond and after another short climb go
down over granite into woods where the trail is
obvious again. Walk by a small lake and farther on
pass a patch of robust lupine, a flower not usually
enjoyed in deep woods. Come to that promised
stand of aspen and then the unbridged stream. Continue in woods to a big granite slab on your right.
Walk up it, at the top resume traveling on an obvious
tread and in a short distance drop for several yards
to the south end of Lake Margaret. Stay right to
reach a good spot for a snack stop. The hike to Lake
Margaret is one of the very few trips in this guide
that doesn't tempt you with additional trails to take.
(The others, all in Lassen Volcanic National Park,
are No's. 1, 2, 7, 9, 10.) Of course, on those—or
any hike—you can make cross-country trips.

Lake Margaret is the lowest and most westerly of
the four hikes in the Carson Pass area (No's. 47
through 50). Despite their proximity, these four are
markedly different from each other in scenery and
mood—a characteristic typical of most trails in the
Sierra. The route to Fourth of July Lake (No. 50)
traverses open slopes, passing several lakes, and
the trail to Showers Lake (No. 48) travels the length
of an immense valley and then returns along the

Caples Creek

48 SHOWERS LAKE

One day trip or backpack
Distance: 5 miles one way
Elevation gain: 660 feet; loss 750 feet
High point: 8,790 feet
Allow 2½ hours one way
Usually open July through October
Topographic maps:
    U.S.G.S. Caples Lake, Calif.
    7.5′   1979
    U.S.G.S. Carson Pass, Calif.
    7.5′   1979

Doing the Showers Lake hike as a loop is one of the most highly recommended trips in this guide. After a short climb to Meiss Pass the trail travels along the floor of an immense, grassy valley unlike any other in the area and then climbs to Showers Lake. The optional return loop follows the crest of the high treeless ridge that forms the southwest wall of the valley. The panorama you'll enjoy includes the terrain you covered on the hike in, views north to Lake Tahoe and landmarks in the Desolation Wilderness and south to the Carson Pass area. A less demanding side trip is the mostly level, 2.0 mile trail to Round Lake (No. 46) that leaves the main route at the 3.0 mile point.

Proceed on California 88 to a big, old wooden sign on the north side of the highway 200 yards west of Carson Pass. (You also can begin on the signed Old Meiss Pass Trail that begins 0.8 mile to the west along 88 but parking is limited here.)

Traverse west on the Pacific Crest Trail, which you'll be following all the way to Showers Lake, from the west side of the parking area. Alternate between gently climbing and descending for 0.9 mile to the junction with the Old Meiss Pass Trail. Stay right and climb in woods and then wind up barren slopes in long, loose switchbacks. Just before Meiss Pass come to a fence and a large pond. Cross the broad crest where you'll have a view of Lake Tahoe and walk through an exceptionally dense patch of wild iris that will be at their blooming best around the first part of August.

Descend to the valley floor, farther on go through a gate and then pass buildings off on your left before another gate. Beyond it come to the signed trail to Round Lake. Stay straight (left) and eventually pass a view of Meiss Lake off to your right and pass the unsigned spur to it. Since it is usually a favorite stomping grounds of the cattle that graze the valley, its shoreline is not a good choice for camping. Have an easy ford the Upper Truckee River and resume traveling on a trail proper instead of the two track route you've been following since below the pass.

Soon come to more woodsy terrain, pass a lake and then a meadow and begin climbing steeply along a slope lush with flowers that peak a week or so later than those iris. Near the end of the climb enter woods, level off and be watching for an unsigned, but obvious, path heading up the open slope on your left. This is the route of the possible return loop. The stream that flows down this slope is a good source of water. Just beyond the junction have a view of Showers Lake directly below, descend and travel along the wooded east side. The remainder of the shore is one-quarter lush vegetation and one-quarter boulders. At the north end come to a sign pointing to Echo Summit. For a view of Dardanelles Lake (No. 46) and Lake Tahoe veer right at the sign post and walk northeast a few hundred feet to the overlook.

The loop will add an extra 1,000 feet of uphill to the return trip and no extra distance. As you climb you'll have a view back to Showers Lake and farther on Round and Meiss Lakes and Lake Tahoe. Walk at a gentle grade and then at a saddle where the main trail drops off to the west stay straight and continue along the crest or on the east (left) side. You'll have a couple brief descents and climbs along the crest and at one point will have to make an extra little climb over a hump because the east slope is a bit steep to contour across. You'll have views of nearby Caples and Woods Lakes, Elephants Back and Round Top south of Carson Pass (No. 50) and the basin holding Emigrant Lake (No. 49). Eventually, you'll be able to see ahead to the pond at Meiss Pass. Study the terrain and pick out the best point to begin angling down to the pass.

Showers Lake

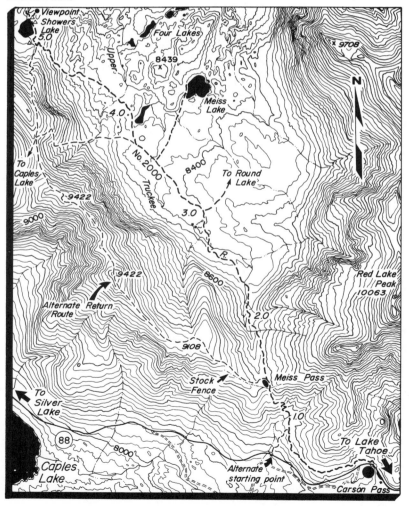

49 EMIGRANT LAKE

One day trip
Distance: 4 miles one way
Elevation gain: 800 feet
High point: 8,600 feet
Allow 2 hours one way
Usually open July through October
Topographic map:
U.S.G.S. Caples Lake, Calif.
7.5'   1979

Emigrant Lake fills the floor of a high walled cirque in the northwesternmost corner of the Mokelumne Wilderness. The trail to it follows the two mile long south shoreline of Caples Lake and then climbs through deep coniferous woods to a dainty meadow just before Emigrant Lake. This is an exceptionally pleasant hike—the distance and elevation gain are just enough to provide a modest workout and the scenery is varied and always attractive. Although this trip will be shown to best advantage in clear weather, since there are no far-ranging views it's also a good choice for a less-than-perfect day.

Drive on California 88 for 5.0 miles west of Carson Pass, passing the beginnings of hikes No's. 48 and 50, or 5.7 miles east of Silver Lake to just below (west of) the spillway at the west end of Caples Lake and a parking area off the south side of the highway. The short hike to Lake Margaret (No. 47) begins 0.2 mile to the west off the north side of the highway.

Climb briefly to lake level and then walk along the wooded shoreline. As a sign off the highway on the north shore relates, the lake was also known as Summit, Clear and Twin Lakes. Dr. James Caples passed the lake on his way to Old Hangtown (Placerville) and then returned to the area to establish a way station that served travelers for 30 years. Pass a marker identifying the route of the Emigrant Road and continue paralleling the lake.

Before you reach the southern tip of the lake travel a bit away from the water's edge and have a series of short climbs and descents. At 2.2 miles have one last view of Caples Lake. Initially head south on the level and then begin climbing in a series of uphill and level sections, like a giant staircase. The steepish portions are always short. Walk beside Emigrant Creek that is lined with willows on the opposite bank and come to a junction. Unfortunately (for hikers at least), construction of the Kirkwood Ski Area eliminated most of the trail to Kirkwood Meadows, the destination given on the post.

Stay straight (left), continue beside the stream for another couple hundred feet before crossing one of its forks with an easy ford. Meander up in woods dotted with rocks, cross Emigrant Creek again, continue up and then make a couple of switchbacks back to near the outlet. Walk through that pretty meadow for the final 0.1 mile to the lake.

A possible return loop for moderately adventurous types would be to turn west onto the truncated trail to Kirkwood Meadows. After a few tenths mile come to a road and a lift. Follow part way up the cleared swath, paralleling the lift, to where you see a small sign on your right marking the route of the Emigrant Road and follow it back to the intersection with the trail along the shore of Caples Lake.

Emigrant Lake

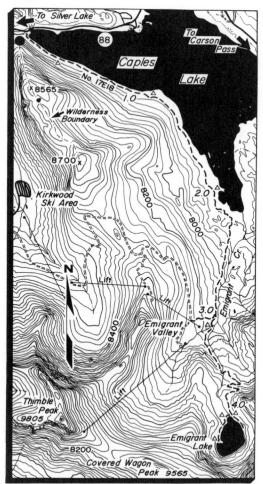

One day trip or backpack
Distance: 4.8 miles one way
Elevation gain: 850 feet; loss 1,350 feet
High point: 9,420 feet
Allow 2½ hours one way
Usually open mid July through October
Topographic maps:
  U.S.G.S. Caples Lake, Calif.
  7.5'   1979
  U.S.G.S. Carson Pass, Calif.
  7.5'   1979

Except for the first one-third mile and the final 1.2 miles, the hike to Fourth of July Lake is along gently inclined, open slopes that initially support a lush covering of grass and an impressive variety of wildflowers and then, as the trail gains a bit of elevation, become more austere, but no less attractive. The trail passes three lakes before the descent to Fourth of July Lake and any one of that trio makes a good stopping point for people wanting a shorter trip. Hikers who are curious about what the destination looks like but don't relish making the climb back out from from Fourth of July Lake can go to a rocky overlook near the 3.8 mile point. However, those wanting extra, not less, work can make the climb of Round Top that would add 1.6 miles round trip and 1,050 feet of uphill.

About 100 yards east of Carson Pass turn south onto a paved road and drive down it 200 feet to signs on the right identifying the Carson Pass Trail and listing mileages to Frog and Fourth of July Lakes

and Ebbetts Pass. If the spaces here are filled you can park off the south side of the highway at Carson Pass.

Wind up at an erratic grade through woods and past boulders for 0.4 mile to a crest and the beginning of those promised gentle slopes. A couple hundred feet farther pass Frog Lake. Climb briefly to the junction of the Pacific Crest Trail, which heads southeast to Ebbetts Pass.

Stay right and traverse along the flank of Elephants Back. Lupine, wyethia and fragrant pennyroyal occupy the most space but scattered among them are a few specimens each of an astounding variety of flowers, including iris, shooting star and columbine. You can see down onto Caples Lake (No. 49), north to nearby Meiss Pass (No. 48) and beyond to Dicks and Jacks Peaks and Mt. Tallac (No. 35), all in the Desolation Wilderness. Continue traversing toward the dark face of Round Top and come to a little crest above Winnemucca Lake.

Drop slightly and stay right where side paths head to the shore until the post marking the more easterly of the two trails down to Woods Lake. Keep straight (left), cross the outlet and climb, crossing a small side stream, along the trail you could see from the crest just above Winnemucca Lake. Descend gently to Round Top Lake and come to the more westerly trail down to Woods Lake. The obvious use path up to Round Top heads left (southeast) from this junction.

To continue to Fourth of July Lake, stay straight and soon cross the outlet from Round Top Lake. Veer away from the lake and begin traveling gradually downhill. Curve left and drop along the west facing slope where you can see the rocky cavern holding Emigrant Lake (No. 49). As you continue farther you'll be looking ahead into the rugged basin of Fourth of July Lake. Turn around for more views of the Desolation area, including Pyramid Peak and the top of the valley holding Echo Lake (No. 38).

If you want to visit the overlook above Fourth of July Lake follow the use path down from the pole supports of a former sign. Near the bottom of the drop bear left—don't climb the little peak—and head up to the edge of the rocks.

From the old sign the main trail begins descending more steeply, switch backs a few times and then heads directly through a rim of sparse timber to the lake, where there are some good campsites.

To make the climb of Round Top take the use path up from Round Top Lake to the saddle just west of the summit block. From here you can understand why Round Top Lake has been called Sock Lake. The rest of the ascent is not difficult or risky until the final few yards. Since the view is quite impressive enough from here, there's no need to do that final portion to the summit.

Fourth of July Lake

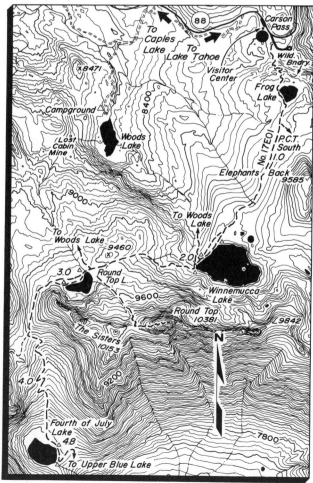

alphabetical listing of trails

*Cover Photos: (top) Mt. Lassen from Brokeoff Mountain
(bottom) Llamas at Meiss Pass*